*President Eisenhower*
*and*
*Strategy Management*

OTHER AFA BOOKS

Collins  *Military Space Forces: The Next 50 Years*
Frisbee  *Makers of the U.S. Air Force*
Mrozek  *Air Power & the Ground War in Vietnam*
Smith  *Assignment: Pentagon—The Insider's Guide to the Potomac Puzzle Palace*
Warden  *The Air Campaign: Planning for Combat*


OTHER AUSA BOOKS

Collins  *Military Space Forces: The Next 50 Years*
Galvin  *The Minute Men: The First Fight—Myths & Realities of the American Revolution*
Matthews & Brown  *The Parameters of Military Ethics*
Matthews & Brown  *The Challenge of Military Leadership*
Smith  *Assignment: Pentagon—The Insider's Guide to the Potomac Puzzle Palace*


OTHER BOOKS BY DOUGLAS KINNARD
*The Secretary of Defense* (1980)
*The War Managers* (1985)


RELATED JOURNALS*
*Armed Forces Journal International*
*Defense Analysis*
*Survival*


*Sample copies available upon request

# President Eisenhower and Strategy Management

## A STUDY IN DEFENSE POLITICS

## Douglas Kinnard

## A Pergamon-Brassey's Classic

Published with
Aerospace Education Foundation
Air Force Association

Published with
Institute of Land Warfare
Association of the U.S. Army

PERGAMON-BRASSEY'S
International Defense Publishers, Inc.

Washington · New York · London · Oxford
Beijing · Frankfurt · São Paulo · Sydney · Tokyo · Toronto

Copyright © 1989 Pergamon-Brassey's International
Defense Publishers, Inc.

First printing 1977, The University of Kentucky Press

Pergamon-Brassey's books are available at special discounts for bulk
purchases for sales promotions, premiums, fund-raising, or education use
through the Special Sales Director, Macmillan Publishing Company
866 Third Avenue, New York, NY 10022.

British Library Cataloguing in Publication Data
Kinnard, Douglas
    President Eisenhower and strategy management : a
    study in defense politics. - (An AFA book) - (An AUSA  book).
    1. United States. Defence. Policies of government, history
    I. Title.
    355'.0335'73
    ISBN 0-08-037434-4


            Library of Congress Cataloging-in-Publication Data
Kinnard, Douglas.
    President Eisenhower and strategy management : a study in defense
    politics / Douglas Kinnard.
        p.  cm. — (An AUSA book)
    Reprint. Originally published: Lexington : University Press of  Kentucky. c1977.
    "Published with Aerospace Education Foundation, Air Force
    Association . . . [and] Institute of Land Warfare, Association of the U.S. Army."
    "A Pergamon-Brassey's classic."
    "An AFA book."
    Bibliography: p.
    Includes index.
    ISBN 0-08-037434-4 : $16.95
    1. United States—Military policy.   2. United States—Politics and
    government—1953–1961.   3. Eisenhower, Dwight David (Dwight David),
    1890–1969.   I. Title.   II. Series.
    [UA23.K482 1989]
    355'.033573—dc20                                             89-33893
                                                                    CIP

Printed in the United States of America

10 9 8 7 6 5 4 3 2 1

# An AFA/AEF Book

The Air Force Association (AFA), established on February 6, 1946, is an independent veterans' organization whose objective is to promote greater understanding of aerospace and national defense issues. On May 1, 1956, AFA established the Aerospace Education Foundation (AEF). The Foundation was established as a nonprofit organization in order to formulate and administer AFA's educational outreach programs.

With a membership of more than 240,000, AFA represents all elements of the Air Force family, military and civilian, active and retired, Reserve and National Guard, cadet and veteran, Civil Air Patrol, civil service, and aerospace workers.

Pergamon-Brassey's AFA Book Series is designed to assist AFA's Aerospace Education Foundation in fulfilling its mandate. AEF's goal is to inform AFA members—and indeed anyone involved in the national defense dialogue—about issues vital to the future of the U.S. Air Force in particular and air power in general. Forthcoming AFA Books may cover the topics of aerospace history, biography, technology, combat, strategy and tactics, personnel, management, leadership, and policy. Publication as an AFA Book does not indicate that the Air Force Association and the publisher agree with everything in the book, but does suggest that the AFA and the publisher believe this book will stimulate the thinking of AFA members and others concerned about important issues.

| U.S.A.<br>(Editorial) | Pergamon-Brassey's International Defense Publishers, Inc., 8000 Westpark Drive, Fourth Floor, McLean, Virginia 22102, U.S.A. |
|---|---|
| (Orders) | Pergamon Press Inc., Maxwell House, Fairview Park, Elmsford, New York 10523, U.S.A. |
| U.K.<br>(Editorial) | Brassey's Defence Publishers Ltd., 24 Gray's Inn Road, London WC1X 8HR, England |
| (Orders) | Brassey's Defence Publishers, Headington Hill Hall, Oxford OX3 OBW, England |
| PEOPLE'S REPUBLIC OF CHINA | Pergamon Press, Room 4037, Qianmen Hotel, Beijing, People's Repulic of China |
| FEDERAL REPUBLIC OF GERMANY | Pergamon Press GmbH, Hammerweg 6, D-6242 Kronberg, Federal Republic of Germany |
| BRAZIL | Pergamon Editora Ltda, Rua Eça de Queiros, 346, CEP 04011, Paraiso, São Paulo, Brazil |
| AUSTRALIA | Pergamon-Brassey's Defence Publishers Ltd., P.O. Box 544, Potts Point, N.S.W. 2011, Australia |
| JAPAN | Pergamon Press, 5th Floor, Matsuoka Central Building, 1-7-1 Nishishinjuku, Shinjuku-ku, Tokyo 160, Japan |
| CANADA | Pergamon Press Canada, Suite No. 271, 253 College Street, Toronto, Ontario, Canada M5T 1R5 |

# An AUSA Institute of Land Warfare Book

The Association of the United States Army, or AUSA, was founded in 1950 as a not-for-profit organization dedicated to education concerning the role of the U.S. Army, to providing material for military professional development, and to the promotion of proper recognition and appreciation of the profession of arms. Its constituencies include those who serve in the Army today, including Army National Guard, Army Reserve, and Army civilians, and the retirees and veterans who have served in the past, and all their families. A large number of public-minded citizens and business leaders are also an important constituency. The Association seeks to educate the public, elected and appointed officials, and leaders of defense industry on crucial issues involving the adequacy of our national defense, particularly those issues affecting land warfare.

In 1988 AUSA established within its existing organization a new entity known as the Institute of Land Warfare. Its purpose is to extend the educational work of AUSA by sponsoring scholarly publications, to include books, monographs, and essays on key defense issues, as well as workshops and symposia. Among the volumes chosen for designation as "An AUSA Institute of Land Warfare Book" are both new texts and reprints of titles of enduring value that are no longer in print. Topics include history, policy issues, strategy, and tactics. Publication as an AUSA Book does not indicate that the Association of the United States Army and the publisher agree with everything in the book, but does suggest that AUSA and the publisher believe this book will stimulate the thinking of AUSA members and others concerned about important issues.

*To Harold Sprout*
*Great Scholar,*
*Great Teacher,*
*Great Friend*

# Contents

# Preface

In reviewing this book on the Eisenhower presidency from the perspective of the late twentieth century, I am struck by the period's continued relevance for those interested in the process of national security policymaking, particularly its undergirding nexus, the strategy-budget dialogue. Granted all historical analogies are unique, still they provide a bedrock of reality on which to discuss the present and to conjecture on the future. Thus those involved in analyzing current defense matters will gain useful insights here.

Moreover, other reasons compel us to take another look at the Eisenhower period when considering current defense issues. The time, the 1950s, is comparatively recent, yet it is well documented—much more so than the Reagan period will be for years to come. The Eisenhower-era issues are also more applicable for the 1990s than comparable examples in the 1960s and 1970s, which were largely driven by the Vietnam War. Most important, *President Eisenhower and Strategy Management* is concerned explicitly with national security policy formulation that emphasizes budgetary constraints, a vital consideration for the military and civilian policymaker alike in the 1990s.

Apropos of the continued relevance of the Eisenhower period to the present time, let me restate the three central conclusions of this book as hypotheses for the present national security environment and then comment briefly under each.

*The defense budget drives national security policy formulation, not vice versa.*

This proposition says the means (the defense budget) determines the ends (national security policy). Theoretically, the president and his senior advisers begin the budget cycle process by deciding what the national security policy should be. This policy is then translated into military requirements and budgets and, after the president's approval, is sent to congress for its action and the eventual appropriation of funds. However, in actual practice the executive budget request is not related directly to policy but to budgetary ceilings which the president decides upon in advance. This process is not wholly without logic; in fact, national security policy is rarely defined with such precision that there can be only one interpretation of the means needed to carry it out.

Thus, for example, in the first Bush defense budget the initial debate was not over strategy at all but over whether the defense budget should reflect a 2 percent real growth (after inflation), as President Reagan had proposed; or a zero real growth (after inflation), President Bush's proposal; or some lesser figure.

*In developing the defense budget, the domestic context is more important than the external context, in time of peace.*

The notion that the domestic context influences policies directed toward external events is not a new one. Thucydides noted how the external behavior of the Greek city states was frequently shaped more by what was happening at home than by actions of the other city states. This concept is particularly relevant to the United States, whose form of government encourages open debate among officials and active involvement of the public.

The present views of the American people reinforce this, giving little reason to believe that external matters will take precedence over domestic problems. In fact, Americans today seem worried that too much attention to national security may be hurting the economy. In 1983, 53 percent of Americans felt that the Reagan defense buildup had been good for the overall economy, while by 1988 the same number felt that the buildup had harmed the economy.

How does all of this square with the forty years of cold war vigilance the United States has been through? While it would be premature to say that the public feels that the cold war is over, few Americans think a growth in defense spending is necessary.

*Process is more important in developing support for national security policies than are the rational arguments for the policies. In this process the president is the prime mover and is the key to mobilizing public opinion on national security issues.*

Let us begin by acknowledging that, given the difference in personalities and the times, especially the present resurgent role of congress, no president in the foreseeable future is going to play the role in deciding national security policy and defense budgets that Eisenhower did in the 1950s. In particular, that any president will have the public image or support on defense issues that General/President Eisenhower did during his White House years is unlikely.

But any president is pivotal in the defense process. It is the president who must make the policy and budgetary case with congress and, more importantly, with the public, if necessary.

It should be emphasized that the defense policy process is highly political in nature. Decisions on defense budgets and national security policy issues, therefore, depend largely on what priority the president gives to defense among competing demands as well as on how well he makes his public case.

At the outset, this book examines the interplay among Ike, his senior military and civilian advisers, and congress in establishing his New Look strategy, technologically heavy and very budget-oriented. The remainder of the book is concerned with how Eisenhower held the line against attacks on his nuclear-heavy strategy and his tight defense budgets from both some of his Joint Chiefs and congress, whose onslaughts were reinforced by a clamor from academia and the media. He was beseiged as well by such external events as Sputnik in 1957 and Khrushchev's Berlin ultimatum in 1958, but Eisenhower managed to hold fast against them all.

There is no end to the lesson here for those who would try to control the strategy-budget dialogue by placing primary emphasis on substantive argument. The reality is that process is more important than substance in achieving strategy-budget outcomes. In the 1950s, the U.S. Air Force won this battle, and the U.S. Army lost. This book tells why.

*Douglas Kinnard*

# Preface
## to the First Edition

There are two schools of thought concerning Eisenhower as president. The conventional one provides the image of a rather weak, though personable, president who relied too much on his subordinates in making important decisions. Generally, this is ascribed to his dislike of the politics of power, which a president must pursue, and to the organizational machinery that he established in the White House to wall himself off from the turmoil. There are, however, great variations in substance, nuance, and methodology among those espousing this view.[1]

The other school of thought, which is by far in the minority and which is not well documented, portrays Eisenhower as a skilled political practitioner. Richard Nixon hinted at it when he said of Eisenhower, "He was a far more complex and devious man than most people realized, and in the best sense of those words." Arthur Larson, another insider in the Eisenhower administration, paints the picture of a strong president who "of all modern Presidents, was the most skillful in building and using the complex administrative structure of the Executive branch in such a way that the President had the fullest benefit of all its resources when making decisions." The most explicit and best-known treatment of Eisenhower as a strong president is Murray Kempton's "The Underestimation of Dwight D. Eisenhower." He was, Kempton writes, "the great tortoise upon whose back the world sat for eight years. We laughed at him; we talked wistfully about moving; and all the while we never knew the cunning beneath the shell." But Kempton's article is essentially undocumented.[2]

This book concerns strategic policymaking during the Eisenhower administration. In particular, it is a study of Eisenhower himself, not in the entire range of his presidential functions, but in his role as strategic manager. It should provide, however, some additional insight on Eisenhower's presidency as a whole.

The early period of the Eisenhower administration has been covered quite well, up through about 1955. The later period has been done less well. However, there are more compelling reasons for writing this book than the extent of previous coverage. Perhaps the most important reason for this study is a wealth of presidential material from the 1955–1960 period made available to me, which has not previously been available to the public. In examining this material I concluded that, contrary to the conventional portrayal of Eisenhower as a passive president, he was, at least in matters of strategic policy-making, very strong indeed. Finally, under the assumption that conclusions from a particular period often have wider relevance and applicability, I believe that additional insight into the Eisenhower presidency might shed some additional light on how United States strategic policy is really made.

Chapter One describes how and why Eisenhower secured his strategic innovation, the New Look, during the years 1953 and 1954. Chapters Two and Three, which contain new documentation, describe how he retained his strategy despite a host of critics outside the government, in Congress, and especially in the military bureaucracy. The focus on Chapters Two and Three is on the years 1956–1959, when Eisenhower was under the most intense pressure to modify his strategy. After 1959, it was too late for Eisenhower to make major changes in strategic policy during his administration. In any case, by 1960 defense issues had merged with the rhetoric of the 1960 election campaign, and that is another story.

The great defense debate of the 1950s has long been of interest to me. I saw it at firsthand, as any army partisan, from the vantage of the army chief of staff's office. Later, I began to try to understand it from the point of view of President Eisenhower. Research for this book began with that interest, but its outcome is quite different than I had anticipated, and for this I want to acknowledge the fine assistance I have received.

I am grateful to John S. D. Eisenhower, whose generous and objective assistance, by way of his time and materials, permitted me to gain an insight from the presidential level which otherwise would not have been possible. I am especially grateful to Professors Robert Gilpin and Harold Sprout of Princeton University for their time, patience, and wisdom, which were of inestimable value in helping me to research for and then write this book. Finally, I would like to acknowledge a special indebtedness to my wife, Wade Tyree Kinnard, for her assistance and encouragement to take the "harder right."

# CHAPTER ONE

# *How the New Look Came to Be*

IT WAS January 20, 1953. From the north portico of the White House and up Pennsylvania Avenue rode the outgoing president, Harry S. Truman, and the first Republican president in twenty years, Dwight David Eisenhower. Eisenhower, bouyant, cheerful, sunny, and on the surface seemingly simple, was a folk hero in his time.

How unbelievable it had all been. From Abilene in the first decade of the twentieth century, Eisenhower had come to West Point in its last years before the Great War as an unknown quantity. Graduating as an average cadet, he was relegated by circumstance to a training role during that war. In the interwar years, he climbed slowly in the isolated military establishment. There were years with General Douglas MacArthur in Washington and Manila and then, at last, with troops as the Second World War began in Europe.

Then came his rise out of obscurity. First he went to Washington to work for George Marshall, who, in those days, was the maker of generals; then to command of the American forces in Europe, followed by Supreme Command of the Allied Expeditionary Forces. Now he was famous and routinely in the company of the great and near great of the allied countries.

Notwithstanding his fame, he was still Ike, with that big smile, increasingly beloved by most Americans. After the war had been won in Europe, he came back to be army chief of staff, usually the capstone of an army career; in this case it was an anticlimax. From Washington, he moved to New York, as president of Columbia University; this was not a good fit for either side. There were rumors that he would run for president, which he denied, of course. The Columbia years were filled with comings and goings on national and international matters not directly related to the university. Numerous wealthy and influential Republicans, generally of a conservative economic outlook, encouraged and nurtured the prospective candidate.

Then duty called again. In the wake of the Korean War which might be part of a worldwide Communist offensive, the North Atlantic Treaty Organization (NATO) needed a supreme commander; they turned to Eisenhower, the old wartime hero. Rumors increased that Eisenhower would run for president; the denials became less sure. In 1952, Eisenhower announced his candidacy. The campaign, which began in disaster in a rainy field in Abilene, ended in a great triumph in November—442 electoral votes to 89 for his opponent, Adlai Stevenson.

Eisenhower's inaugural address was comparatively short, devoted almost exclusively to foreign policy matters. There was only passing reference to domestic issues. The next day many newspapers noted that Eisenhower's message was a repudiation of isolationism. It was that, certainly, and it was also a message to the Taft wing of the Republican party that the party must revise its traditional isolationist views and relate more to a changing world.

If there were potential differences between the new president and the conservative wing of his party on international matters, there were few differences on their economic outlooks.[1] Both were conservative, which meant they both supported reduced and balanced budgets and hoped to reduce taxes.[2] A balanced budget, at that time, was almost entirely dependent on cuts in the defense portion, which accounted for about 70 percent of the federal budget.

On April 30, 1953, the Eisenhower team met at the White House to go over Truman's proposed budget for fiscal year 1954 and to make some revisions. The meeting was chaired by President Eisenhower and attended by certain members of his cabinet, as well as by Republican legislative leaders. Strong emphasis was placed on the national defense portion of the budget, where it was pointed out that while reductions had been made from the Truman estimates, there would still have to be heavy military spending, and, therefore, the new administration could not expect to balance this first budget. As was reported later, "When this hit Robert A. Taft, he went off like a bomb, . . . fairly shouting and banging his fist on the Cabinet table. . . . 'The one primary thing we promised the American people,' he shouted, 'was reduction of expenditures. Now you're taking us right down the same road Truman traveled. It's a repudiation of everything we promised in the campaign.' "[3]

Eisenhower was a newcomer to politics and to the Republican party. Robert Taft was "Mr. Republican" himself and had been Eisenhower's adversary for the Republican nomination. Taft was Republican leader of the Senate, and the president felt dependent upon his support in that body. Although Eisenhower's immense popularity had been an important factor in his election, the two major pledges of his campaign were also of great importance: to end the Korean War and to reduce the role of the federal government in American life. Although this latter point was perhaps more effective as rhetoric than as a guide to economic policy, its real intent was reduced and balanced budgets.

Immediately after his nomination in Chicago, Eisenhower had visited his defeated rival, Taft, and had said of him, "His willingness to cooperate is absolutely necessary to the success of the Republican Party in the campaign and in the administration to follow." The formal negotiations for cooperation in the campaign took place at the famous breakfast meeting between Taft and Eisenhower at 60 Morningside Drive, New York City, on September 12, 1952. To the meeting Taft had brought a statement of understanding of Eisenhower's philosophy on a number of issues. This statement included the objective of reducing the federal budget to $70 billion for fiscal year 1954 (from the current rate of $74 billion) and to $60 billion in fiscal year 1955. Eisenhower said later, "This goal seemed reasonable, although perhaps too ambitious in timing." [4]

In light of the foregoing, the president felt "obligated to redeem promises made in the Republican platform of 1952, to keep pledges I had made in the campaign, and to follow through on the recommendations submitted in my State of the Union message." [5]

One important promise concerned the liquidation of the Korean War. By mid-1952, the Korean War had been in a stalemate for a year. Eisenhower's campaign pledge to end the war was highly appealing to the American public and had to be redeemed for purely domestic reasons. The international implications of ending the war were also favorable. Any reduction in the military forces, which would be necessary to curtail defense budget outlays, depended upon an early end to hostilities. There was, therefore, a direct relationship between Eisenhower's two major campaign promises, ending the war and reducing the budget.

Eisenhower had pledged in Detroit on October 24, 1952, in the most dramatic speech of his campaign, that if elected he would personally go to Korea to end the war. Less than a month after his election he set out for the Far East. This trip reinforced Eisenhower's determination to terminate the war one way or another. The president decided to continue with the truce discussions at Panmunjom, which had begun in July 1951. If these talks were to succeed, both sides would have to understand that a termination of the war was in their self-interest. As Eisenhower himself said, "Because you know, my friends, just because one side wants peace doesn't make peace. We must go ahead and do things that induce the others to want peace also." In the perception of the new president, this was to be achieved as follows:

"One possibility was to let the Communist authorities understand that, in the absence of satisfactory progress, we intended to move decisively without inhibition in our use of weapons, and would no longer be responsible for confining hostilities to the Korean Peninsula. We would not be limited by any worldwide gentleman's agreement. In India and in the Formosa Straits area, and at the truce negotiations at Panmunjom, we dropped the word, discreetly, of our intention. We felt quite sure it would reach Soviet and Chinese ears. Soon the prospects for Armistice negotiations seemed to improve." [6]

The administration took other psychological and military actions, but because there were some major international events of potential relevance, such as the death of Joseph Stalin, there is no way of knowing what was decisive in ending the war. On Sunday evening, July 26, 1953, the president was able to redeem his most dramatic campaign pledge when he broadcast to the nation from the White House that the Korean War was over.

The importance of the war's termination is threefold. First, by keeping his campaign pledge promptly, the president's public image and appeal were even more enhanced. Second, the way was cleared for a reduction in U.S. military forces and a new strategic approach. Finally, this new approach could clear the way for reduced budgets and possibly reduced taxes, a major element of the Republican program.[7]

It soon became evident, however, that any immediate reduction in the defense portion of the budget could be achieved only by deferring certain expenditures to another fiscal year because the Joint Chiefs of Staff were unable, or possibly unwilling, to accept any reduction of current force goals. In May 1953 the administration forwarded to Congress a revision of the final Truman budget, in which all the services received some reductions, and the air force received more than the others. This set off a critical reaction from congressional Democrats, most notably Senator Stuart Symington, former air force secretary. The administration's position, as reflected by the defense secretary and his deputy, was that the cut was the result of improved management and reflected no change in strategic policy. Although this was contested by the outgoing air force chief of staff, Hoyt S. Vandenberg, in the end the administration's position was carried.[8] The resulting budget was more than $6 billion under the Truman estimates. Neither the administration nor the Republican congressional leaders were satisfied with the extent of the cut. It was evident, however, that any major cuts in the future could not be achieved by management improvements, but would require some type of strategic innovation that would permit a reduction in force goals.

No administration begins completely anew in formulating its strategic policy. Whatever its differences in outlook from its predecessor, it inherits an existing strategic policy when it assumes office. In order to understand Eisenhower's strategic innovations, we must look at the Truman legacy, beginning with the document NSC-68, developed in early 1950. The origins, drafting, and significance of NSC-68 have been exhaustively covered by Paul Y. Hammond.[9]

Document NSC-68 had its origins in the perceptions of American leaders concerning Soviet strategic posture and foreign policy and in the presidential decision of January 30, 1950, to initiate the hydrogen bomb project. Appended to the document initiating the H-bomb project was a letter, drafted in the State Department, which directed an overall review of U.S. foreign and defense policy. This review subsequently culminated in NSC-68.

In its analysis of the threat to the United States, the document concluded that the USSR aspired to world hegemony, after consolidating its own power base in the Soviet Union and its satellites. The paper pictured an inherent conflict between the United States and the USSR, since the former was a threat to the latter's objectives. On the technical level, it estimated that by 1954 the USSR would have sufficient atomic bombs and means of delivery to offset significantly the U.S. nuclear capability. The paper ruled out any prospects of regulating armaments and any possibility of negotiating with the Soviet Union except from a position of strength. The chief limitations in American power were viewed as a lack of conventional military forces and the military and economic weaknesses of Western Europe. The document concluded with a strong call for a much greater commitment of U.S. resources to national security.

During the spring of 1950, before the North Korean attack, the Truman administration was trying to balance its economic prospects with the larger effort proposed by NSC-68. What the outcome would have been is not clear. As events turned out, action on NSC-68 merged with the Korean War rearmament, although the document itself was unapproved and unprogrammed when the war began. The document provided the base of assumptions for the great expansion of U.S. forces and their deployment to Asia and Europe during the Korean War.

There is another element of the Truman strategic legacy to be considered. In the summer of 1952, the president directed a study that would portray to the new administration strategic problems and appropriate implementing programs. This was, in effect, a revision of NSC-68 and was subsequently numbered NSC-141. It was, apparently, a type of "dream" paper in which an outgoing group recommends expensive programs which it would never undertake itself. The practical effect of the document was negligible, since its thrust toward larger defense expenditure was contrary to the views of the incoming administration.

In December 1952 President-elect Eisenhower returned to Hawaii from his promised visit to Korea aboard the United States Navy cruiser *Helena*. During this voyage his companions included certain secretarial level and other high-ranking officials from the incoming administration. Views on the significance of the discussions that took place aboard the *Helena* vary, but it is generally agreed that in addition to the Korean War, overall matters of defense policy, foreign policy, and the economy were on the agenda. The election was over, and it was now time to come to grips with what Eisenhower called the "great equation": specifically, how to maintain an adequate defense policy, meet domestic requirements, and still obtain the budgetary and tax reductions inherent in the Republican views on managing the economy. One notion growing out of these discussions that had implications in the defense area was the "long haul." [10]

This was first announced by the president in a press conference in April 1953 as follows: "We reject the idea that we must build up to a maximum attainable strength for some specific date theoretically fixed for a specified time in the future. Defense is not a matter of maximum strength for a single date. It is a matter of adequate protection to be projected as far into the future as the actions and apparent purposes of others may compel us. It is a policy that can, if necessary, be lived with over a period of years." [11] Elsewhere in the conference the president referred to this as a "radical change in policy." The change he was referring to was from the Truman administration's concept of the "year of maximum danger."

The idea of a critical year originated in the study that produced NSC-68. In early 1950 it appeared that for a combination of technological, production, and modernization reasons, the Soviet Union's military capability would peak in 1954, which then became the crisis year. However, quite apart from that estimate, the actual function of a crisis year was as a guide for planning and programming. Since different elements of an integrated military force take varying times to complete their preparations, a target date permits an orderly phasing of these elements. There is no point in having the ship ready before the sailors, or vice versa.

The president, however, was interpreting the crisis year in another way for his own reasons. He was saying that there was no "magic" year of crisis, but rather that the Soviet threat would last over many years and that, therefore, so should our preparations to meet that threat. What he had in mind probably can be viewed in two different ways. On the one hand, he wanted to avoid alternate buildups and drops in military expenditures, with the resulting probability of economic dislocation. Another, and probably more pertinent, objective was psychological. By removing the idea of a crisis year, with its attendant sense of urgency, and substituting the idea of a "long haul," that is, a permanent program, the scope of armament could be curtailed and its pace slowed. Viewed this way, it may simply have been a rationale for stretching out military requirements.

About a week before the president's press conference, the NATO Council had met in Paris and was informed by Dulles of the notion of the long haul. The concept was accepted in NATO strategic planning almost immediately. Since both the British and French were having their own problems in meeting the NATO force goals, they were sympathetic to the idea. The result was NATO adoption of a similar approach, which would "preserve and not exhaust" the economic strength of the member nations.[12]

Adoption of the long haul did not in itself constitute a new strategic policy. It provided a convenient rationale for programming force development and force modernization over a longer period of time. In itself, however, this change did not foreclose several alternative strategic policies that the new administration could have chosen in 1953. More important in developing the new strategic policy were certain convictions that Eisenhower apparently held when he became president. These he called "basic considerations" that provided "logical guidelines for designing and employing a security establishment." They are quoted below in part:

> I had long been convinced that the composition and structure of our military establishment should be based on the assumption that the U.S. on its own initiative would never start a major war. . . . Nevertheless the assumption did not, in my view, presuppose that America's response to attack would have to accord with the exact nature of aggression. . . .
>
> America's forces must be designed primarily to deter a conflict, even though they might be compelled later to fight.
>
> The relationship . . . between military and economic strength is intimate and indivisible. What America needed, I felt, was a fully adequate military establishment headed by men of sufficient breadth of view to recognize and sustain appropriate relationships among the moral, intellectual, economic, and military facets of our strength. . . .
>
> They would, of course, have to realize that the diabolical threat of international Communism . . . would be with us for decades to come.
>
> Our armed forces must be modern.

The logical role of our allies along the periphery of the Iron Curtain, therefore, would be to provide (with our help) for their own local security, especially ground forces, while the United States, centrally located and strong in productive power, provided mobile reserve forces of all arms, with emphasis on sea and air contingents.[13]

Eisenhower's strategic concept may be summarized as follows: to rely on deterrence and rule out preventive war; to stress the new technology; to place heavy reliance on allied land forces around the Soviet periphery; to stress economic strength, achieved especially through reduced defense budgets; and to be prepared to continue the struggle with communism over decades.

In the first six months of the new administration, there were a series of events potentially important to Soviet-American relationships that make the period a kind of bench mark for students of foreign policy: the death of Stalin in March, the Korean armistice in July, and the successful testing of the first Soviet hydrogen device in August. It seems doubtful, however, that the U.S. leaders viewed these events as providing major opportunity for foreign policy initiatives at the time. The new administration, even aside from its anti-Communist views as set forth in the 1952 Republican campaign, inherited years of mutual distrust between the United States and the Soviet Union. This long-standing distrust conditioned the nature and depth of the leaders' perceptions on both sides. The American view seemed to be that at most there had been a change in the style or tactics of Stalin's successors, but not in their objectives.

As the U.S. leaders saw Soviet military capabilities, the USSR, with its large land mass, had interior lines and a formidable ground army, which at that time was oriented toward Europe both in composition and deployment. Substantial elements of the Soviet army were stationed in Eastern Europe. The Soviet navy was working toward first-class status, but was not yet in the category of the United States Navy. Soviet tactical air forces were extensive, but also had an extensive perimeter to defend. The Soviet strategic air force had perhaps 200 atomic weapons,[14] with aircraft that could be employed against Western Europe, but which were not yet capable of reaching the United States. And in August 1953 the first successful Soviet fusion weapon was exploded. In sum, although by 1953 the preponderance of strategic forces were on the side of the United States, the same could not be said in terms of other military forces capable of employment in Europe or other places on the Eurasian land mass.

The new administration's views on the nature of Russia's threat to the United States can be traced to the presidential campaign. The author of the foreign policy plank for the 1952 Republican campaign was John Foster Dulles. By 1952 Dulles had expressed some rather definite ideas on the Communist threat. In a December 1950 speech he used what was for him a familiar theme: "By these methods the Russian State and the Bolshevik Party, working hand in hand, brought about 800 million people under their control. . . . And still they are rolling on toward their goal of a Communist world. Who was there to stop them?"[15] His answer was the United States. The American people had responded, but much remained to be done, and he hoped eventually for a "righteous peace." Dulles spoke and wrote extensively, especially on matters of foreign affairs, always conscious of what he perceived to be the Soviet Union's long-term strategy of "encirclement and strangulation" of the United States.

Shortly after the White House announced on April 11, 1952, Eisenhower's forthcoming departure from the military, the general wrote a letter to Dulles commenting on an article Dulles had prepared for *Life* magazine. There was one aspect of the article that bothered Eisenhower. "What should we do if Soviet political aggression . . . successively chips away exposed portions of the free world? . . . To my mind this is the case where the theory of 'retaliation' falls down."[16] Perhaps of greater interest are those portions of Dulles's article which pertain to the threat posed by the USSR and with which the prospective presidential candidate presumably agreed. A few excerpts should convey Dulles's perceptions of the Soviet threat. The introduction begins, "Soviet Communism confronts our nation with its gravest peril." Then, in criticism of the policies of the Democratic administration, he stated, "Our present negative policies will never end the type of sustained offensive which Soviet Communism is mounting; they will never end the peril." At one point Dulles invoked natural law against the Soviet leaders: "There is a moral or natural law not made by man which determines right and wrong and in the long run only those who conform to that law will escape disaster. This law has been trampled by the Soviet rulers, and for that violation they can and should be made to pay." [17]

In the same month Dulles wrote Eisenhower of an interesting development based upon a call he had received from Robert Taft. According to Dulles, Taft stated that he was in agreement with Dulles's speeches and writings on foreign policy. Further, he felt that Dulles might prepare a draft foreign policy plank for the Republican platform on behalf of both Taft and Eisenhower. The final platform, which eventually received the blessing of the two major candidates, was primarily an attack on Democratic mismanagement in the field of foreign policy. The thrust was that by blunders and betrayal, the Truman administration had given "Communist Russia a military and propaganda initiative which, if unstayed, will destroy us." In addition, the platform said, the gains of Communist Russia had been so great, again because of the blundering of the Democratic administration, that it "proceeds confidently with its plan for world conquest." [18]

When Eisenhower assumed office, the United States was a party to three multilateral and one bilateral defense treaties and two defensive arrangements by executive agreement.[19] The most important of these obligations was the North Atlantic Treaty Organization. NATO, with which the new president was quite familiar, was in its third phase of political-military development by the early days of the Eisenhower administration.

From its founding in April 1949 until the outbreak of the Korean War, there was an ambivalence between the conflicting objectives of an ambitious strategic concept entailing costly armaments and the domestic economic objectives of countries still in the process of recovering from World War II. From the point of view of many European officials, the American commitment to the defense of Western Europe against the USSR in 1949 was of value primarily because it placed Europe under the protection of U.S. strategic weapons. Even after the first Russian atomic explosion in August 1949, there seemed to be no sense of urgency in meeting the agreed force goals to support the strategic concept, which had been endorsed by the North Atlantic Council in January of that year. This confidence seemed to be based on the assumption that the U.S. atomic capability would deter the USSR from any military attack on Western Europe, and, therefore, Western Europe might proceed on her most important project, economic recovery, with only minimal efforts toward rearmament.[20]

The outbreak of the Korean War in June 1950 began the second phase of NATO's development. To some people, the war in Korea at first appeared not as a unique event, but rather as part of an overall Soviet strategy involving war by proxy, which could be employed elsewhere including, perhaps, Europe.[21] Also, whatever the motive or meaning of the war might be, there was always the possibility of its spreading to other parts of the world. It was perhaps more immediately pertinent that the war undermined the assumption previously held by NATO countries that the U.S. atomic arsenal would be a deterrent to Soviet-sponsored military action. We know now that Korea turned out to be unique, but at the time it seemed clear that a Soviet-sponsored military action had not been deterred by the United States. Could it be assumed that the deterrent would be more successful elsewhere?

Such, then, was the atmosphere when the North Atlantic Council met in New York in September 1950. On the evening before the meeting, President Truman pledged substantial increases in U.S. forces to be stationed in Europe in exchange for European development of their own force levels.[22] At the meeting the council explicitly adopted a "forward strategy" and initiated an examination of how Germany, without whose assistance any forward strategy would be meaningless, could make its contribution to European defense. Other significant actions included agreement to establish an integrated force and a supreme commander (who would, it was generally understood, be an American). The Korean War had, in a matter of months, transformed NATO from a kind of mutual defense treaty into a multinational military organization soon to have its own command arrangements. In the course of this transformation the European resource commitments to the alliance were substantially increased.

By the summer of 1951, however, the Korean War had reached a stalemate, and it began to appear to be a unique event rather than one element of a larger pattern of Soviet aggression. The result was an increased confidence in the U.S. deterrent and a failure on the part of the Europeans to meet the new force levels they had pledged when they had adopted a forward strategy the year before. As one expert put it, "although the gap between strategy and capabilities was somewhat narrowed, the disparity between the pledged and actual contributions to NATO was greatly enlarged." [23]

Given Eisenhower's strategic views and the domestic and international constraints he perceived, his problem was to blend those views into a credible strategy that could be implemented at a relatively low cost and be sold to both the American public and American allies. To accomplish this objective, the president used organizational means, careful selection of key political appointees, his large experience in handling bureaucracies, and his great rapport with the American people. The personalities of his lieutenants were important, as was the process of strategic policy-making he oversaw: the interrelationships of the decision makers, departments, and agencies responsible for U.S. national security.

At the apex of the defense and foreign policy organization, Eisenhower established a refurbished National Security Council (NSC). Originally the NSC was created by Congress as a small advisory body over which the president was to preside.[24] Under Truman the council had been rather loosely structured. Eisenhower transformed this loose framework into a highly structured system.

Soon after taking office, Eisenhower indicated the kind of council he wanted to Robert Cutler, who subsequently became special

assistant for national security affairs. One presidential requirement was the need for continuous policy planning to be done by
a planning board as the "planning arm" of the NSC. He also
wanted wider representation in the council, including the secretary of the treasury and the budget director. Eisenhower viewed
the council as a "corporate body," that is, the members not only
represented their departments but could give advice in their own
right. Procedures were also to be established so that meetings
would follow a standard pattern, including an advance agenda
and advance circulation of policy papers to be considered.[25]

The substructure that Cutler developed to support the council had an input board and an output board. For input there was
established a Planning Board (known as the NSC "Senior Staff"
under Truman), which Cutler chaired and whose members (at
the assistant secretary level) came from departments represented
on the council. The functions of the board, which was in fact an
interagency committee, were to draw up the agenda for each
council meeting and to put in final form policy papers for council consideration. On the output side there was created the Operations Coordinating Board (OCB), initially chaired by the
undersecretary of state. It also was an interagency committee, but
at the undersecretary level. Its function was to follow through
on presidential policy decisions by transmitting them to the implementing departments and to feed back to the president progress reports on policy implementation.

During the first two years of the Eisenhower administration
the council met weekly. The president was always briefed in advance on the policy papers to be considered. These papers followed a fixed format and contained, when appropriate, a financial impact appendix. Following the meeting, a record of action
was forwarded to the president, which upon approval became
the basis for OCB follow-through. The meetings themselves began
with a CIA briefing, following which Cutler would brief the first
agenda item and then act as moderator for the discussion. Eisenhower served as chairman and took a very active part in the
meetings. Lively exchanges apparently were not unusual. Accord-

ing to one regular observer, Eisenhower was much more forceful in the meetings than Truman had been and appeared much more independent of Dulles than Truman had been of Acheson.[26]

The most important policy paper output of the NSC system was the annual Basic National Security Policy (BNSP) paper. This document was rather broad in nature and "defined U.S. interests and objectives, analyzed the major trends in world affairs that might affect them, and set forth a national strategy for achieving them, covering political, economic, and military elements thereof."[27] Developing the annual BNSP paper required extensive staffing throughout the departments and was the occasion for a good deal of skillful wordsmithing. The importance of this document was that a large number of more detailed policy papers were prepared using it as a starting point. Because of its scope and the number of bureaucratic interests involved, the planning board sometimes took two to three months to complete the annual revision.

Not all defense matters came to the president through the NSC system. If a defense issue did not involve the formulation, revision, or clarification of an NSC policy, then it was not part of the NSC system. These matters were handled by the staff secretary (who was also the defense liaison officer) directly with the president. Procedures might involve informal briefings by Brigadier General Andrew J. Goodpaster on operational or intelligence matters or meetings with cabinet officials or others, which Goodpaster normally attended. Apparently the number of such meetings on defense-related matters was rather substantial. At least one well-placed observer, who was present at nearly all the National Security Council meetings during the last twenty-seven months of the administration, felt that the informal office meetings were much more important than the council sessions: "As a matter of fact, I think the Boss regarded both the Cabinet and the National Security Council meetings as debating societies. . . . His real decisions were in the Oval Room, with a small select group."[28]

This latter point puts a rather different perspective on the

conventional critique of the Eisenhower National Security Council system, the most quoted source of which is Senator Henry
Jackson's subcommittee report. This subcommittee felt that the
Eisenhower NSC was too large a group with too crowded an
agenda and that its procedures were too stylized to be effective.
What the subcommittee overlooked was that Eisenhower was, in
most instances, using the NSC meetings as a coordinating device
and as a forum to announce decisions, rather than to make
them.[29]

President Eisenhower's selection of John Foster Dulles as his
secretary of state was not inevitable, but it was not surprising.
Dulles had campaigned and worked long and hard for the office,
and his talents for such a position were considerable. Dulles had
spent most of his life as a highly successful Wall Street lawyer,
specializing in international cases. In 1944 he became presidential candidate Thomas Dewey's chief adviser on foreign policy.
This role started for him an association with government that
was to continue for the remainder of his life. At the United Nations San Francisco Conference in 1945 he became directly involved in diplomatic practice. By the late 1940s he was the
unofficial foreign policy spokesman for the Republican party.
Dewey's defeat in 1948 cost Dulles the job of secretary of state at
that time, but the Truman administration, in efforts at a bipartisan foreign policy, employed him extensively. Perhaps his most
important assignment for Truman was as chief U.S. negotiator of
the Japanese peace treaty in 1951.

Dulles's views on foreign affairs were well known through two
books and many articles and speeches, activities that he began in
earnest about 1936. There was a heavy Calvinistic component to
Dulles's thinking and articulation, which went back to his child-
hood. Such a style, combined with his perceptions of the Communist threat, resulted in a significant escalation of the cold war
rhetoric.[30] Apparently Stalin's "Problems of Leninism," which
Dulles took seriously as a Soviet program for action, was the
source he used most frequently for his notions on the threat of
"atheistic Communism."

The long years as a lawyer in New York had also left their mark on the Dulles personality, both in his method of approaching problems and in his articulation of solutions. If there is one common theme in the Princeton oral history transcripts of Dulles's former colleagues in the cabinet or NSC, it concerns Dulles's characteristic of being able to present a tight, well-reasoned, and well-argued case in the manner of a good lawyer. It was a source of his influence with his associates and in his relationship with the president.

The relationship between Eisenhower and his new secretary of state had not been close prior to the 1952 election. There seems to be a general consensus among observers at cabinet and NSC meetings that in the early days of the administration, Dulles was very cautious in his dealings with the president. As time went on the relationship altered, however, and by 1954 or so it became a close one. As Sherman Adams points out, Dulles was the only cabinet official who routinely used his right of direct access to the president's office. Apparently many of these visits came late in the day and led into philosophical discussions once business had been disposed of.[31]

It seems abundantly clear from his memoirs that Eisenhower had a high regard for Dulles's capabilities, and this seems borne out by those in a position to observe. There seems also to be no doubt that Dulles was one of the two or three most influential presidential advisers. At this point a note of caution seems in order. There grew up a mythology in the 1950s which has not been entirely dispelled, namely, that U.S. foreign policy of that period was that of John Foster Dulles. The president, this view holds, delegated major policy matters to Dulles. Close research does not bear out this view.[32] Perhaps the relationship can better be summed up in the words of one of Dulles's personal assistants. "He [Dulles] felt that the Secretary of State really was the President's lawyer for foreign affairs. . . . He thought the relationship was very like a lawyer and client, and that his job was to advise and counsel, but basically on behalf of his client who ultimately had the authority and the power."[33]

The president's "Chief of Staff," Sherman Adams, felt that all in all Dulles was the most successful of the cabinet officials in selling his point to the others, even where there was disagreement on basic policy. This was no doubt due in part to his powers of persuasion, but it was also due in part to a proclivity to stay out of what he considered to be others' areas of competence. Nowhere is this better illustrated than in what Dulles regarded as the purely military area. No doubt the military background and reputation of the president were basic reasons for this. Whatever the reason, this lack of involvement is significant, since military force played such a large part in his policies, writings, and speeches when he was secretary of state.[34]

Another cabinet officer with considerable influence was the secretary of the treasury, George Magoffin Humphrey. The United States Treasury is a powerful institution, at the center of domestic and international struggles concerning financial, fiscal, and tax policies. It takes a relatively weak man to underplay the role of secretary of the treasury, considering the large domestic and international clientele who have a stake in his approaches and policies. With the advent of the Eisenhower administration, the importance of the job was even more evident. The Republican campaign had stressed and promised balanced budgets, debt and tax reductions, and fiscal and monetary checks on inflation.

Humphrey was first suggested to Eisenhower by Lucius Clay some time after the election. Clay recommended him as an able administrator who was dedicated to sound fiscal and financial policies and who was impeccable in integrity and character.[35] Humphrey was sixty-three when he came to Washington as Eisenhower's secretary of treasury. His career, which began as a lawyer, had been almost entirely with the M. A. Hanna Corporation of Cleveland, where by 1952 he was chairman of the board. M. A. Hanna was one of the country's largest industrial-holding companies, being involved in steel, iron, coal, ore, and other kinds of enterprises.

Humphrey arrived in Washington with a "passion for domestic economy and dispassion toward foreign affairs." He was, in keeping with his background, highly conservative on economic issues. He seems to have been extremely vigorous in NSC sessions, into which he frequently interspersed short talks on checking deficits. Many of those who had an opportunity to observe him remarked on his personal charm, warmth, and vitality. Of great importance to him in cabinet meetings was his debating skill, overpowering manner, and conviction, which permitted him to overwhelm most of his colleagues.[36]

The president apparently thought highly of Humphrey from the outset, and this regard increased as time went on. Early in his administration, Eisenhower added the secretary of treasury as a regular member of the National Security Council. It was in this forum that Humphrey probably exerted his most direct influence on matters of national security policy. Robert Sprague, a sometime consultant to the NSC, comments on Humphrey's role as follows: "I'll go so far as to say that by all odds at the meetings of the NSC that I attended, except for the President, Mr. Humphrey's was the strongest personality, and had the strongest influence."[37]

It would be a mistake, though, to conclude that Eisenhower accepted Humphrey's proposals uncritically. Sherman Adams pointed out that, notwithstanding Eisenhower's great respect for Humphrey, the president felt that he was too simplistic in equating problems of government and private industry and "occasionally too impatient for fast action."[38]

Charles E. Wilson, the secretary of defense, like the treasury secretary, was suggested to the president by Lucius Clay. Wilson was the highly successful president of General Motors who exhibited a powerful and confident personality. Bluff and colorful in manner, he was prone to making highly quotable statements of a type not designed to enhance his relations with Congress. When he arrived at the Pentagon, his insight into foreign affairs or strategic issues was negligible, and he did not seem to gain much sophistication as time went on.

Wilson, in the view of many observers, was inclined to overtalk situations with the president and to bring to Eisenhower too many internal problems of the Defense Department. Apparently his presentations were also frequently so rambling that the president became impatient. As time went on, "Engine Charlie," as he was known, declined in influence with the president, while the other two powerful men in the cabinet, Dulles and Humphrey, greatly increased their influence.[39]

Operating at the juncture of the military and the higher political authority is the chairman of the Joint Chiefs of Staff. His effectiveness is highly dependent on his relationships with the secretary of defense and the president. Admiral Arthur Radford, whom the president-elect had given Wilson an opportunity to "look over" during the Korean trip, was Wilson's choice for chairman. Radford subsequently gained great influence with the secretary of defense and became very highly regarded by President Eisenhower.[40]

Radford's predecessor, Omar Bradley, although a political spokesman for the Truman administration, had generally maintained a position of neutrality on matters of interservice conflict. Radford, however, was another sort of person. When he had been vice chief of naval operations during the interservice controversies of the late 1940s, he had been a ruthless partisan and outstanding bureaucratic infighter. These talents he brought with him to the chairman's job. Far from assuming a position of neutrality, Radford took positions on written documents and during NSC meetings and other discussions. Since he normally represented the military in meetings with the president, the NSC, and the secretary of defense, he was in a position to wield considerable power. Articulate, personable, and in sympathy with the president's outlook on budgetary and strategic questions, he was someone to be reckoned with in the 1950s. He had a close rapport with Dulles, overshadowed Wilson on strategic matters, and had the confidence of the president.[41]

The uniformed chiefs of the army, air force, and navy each had three primary sources of bureaucratic power: his role in the joint arena, his role as the chief military officer of an organization with a worldwide infrastructure of personnel and facilities, and his role as a service chief in the budgetary process. The first role provided some potential opportunities to influence national security policy. It was to the second role, however, that the chief of staff normally devoted the bulk of his time, and from which he derived his greatest influence not only within his own service but also with the Congress, special interest groups, and the public. The third source of power, his service budget, was a recurring administrative process of great importance in determining strategic policy outcomes.

The service chief who has spent his entire adult life in the military service represents his agency in a manner in which no political appointee possibly could. He is the essence of the military professional and in this role usually considers himself apolitical.[42] He is also the father of his service and there to protect it and its budget as best he can.

Matthew B. Ridgway, Eisenhower's successor at SHAPE, was the president's choice for army chief of staff. Ridgway, fifty-eight years old, was well known, especially in his command of the Eighth Army in Korea and as MacArthur's successor in Japan. Since the Korean War had only recently ended when Ridgway assumed office, one of his pressing planning problems concerned the army's personnel strength in the future. The peacetime army had always been small, although it was larger before the Korean War than before World War II. But Ridgway understood the situation in 1952 to be different from that before Korea. First, he saw an increasingly sophisticated Soviet militar[y threa]t. Second, he saw constantly increasing U.S. military comm[itments t]o other countries. Finally, he did not agree that heavy re[liance o]n a nuclear weapons capability was adequate to meet [i]t. Regarding this latter point, his was the long-standing [pos]ition that the man on ground, the foot soldier, wa[s the deci]sive element.[43]

Eisenhower's selection for air force chief of sta[ff], Nathan F. Twining, began his new role with a distinct advantage over the other service chiefs, since that service's strategic concepts, which stressed the central importance of the strategic deterrent, were highly congenial to the new administration. Before Twining's arrival there had been a heated dispute between the outgoing air force chief, Hoyt Vandenberg, and the new administration. This was not over strategic concepts, however, but whether the old Truman goal of 143 air force wings by fiscal year 1955 or the new Eisenhower goal of 120 wings would be sufficient. Eisenhower had prevailed, but the dispute possibly accelerated Twining's assumption of his new position about six weeks before the other chiefs.[44]

Admiral Robert B. Carney was Eisenhower's selection to be chief of naval operations. The navy's strategic concepts were somewhere between those of the army and the air force and were based upon two principles: control of the sea commensurate with needs, and the ability to deny its use to unfriendly or inimical nations.[45]

As to how control was to be maintained, the navy believed in a variety of capabilities, of which atomic warfare was only one element. The navy stressed its versatility, while placing greatest emphasis on fast carrier task forces, with their mobility, staying power, and the punishing capability of their air component at sea or at distant land points. The navy, in the pre-Polaris days, also stressed the nuclear delivery capability of aircraft launched from carriers and capable of striking the USSR.

By July 1953 it was time to take a new look at the United States' strategic policy. The president initiated this in a meeting with the new chiefs, who were to be sworn in the following month. Since the Korean armistice was about to be signed, the president wanted to develop a defense posture that could be continued for the indefinite future. He wanted the new chiefs, before they were immersed in their offices, to agree on a paper on overall defense policy. This was only the first step in what subsequently became known as the New Look, which the president later defined as "first a reallocation of resources among the five categories of forces, and second, the placing of greater emphasis than formerly on the deterrent and destructive power of improved nuclear weapons, better means of delivery, and effective air-defense units."[47] The president's idea was to separate the chiefs from their staffs and encourage them to work on their own.

In early August, the chiefs took a four-day cruise down the Potomac on the secretary of the navy's yacht, the *Sequoia*. As Radford tells it, by the fourth day most were anxious to get home, and unanimity developed on a basic paper of strategic premises and guidelines.[48]

Translating these generalities into specifics for the fiscal year 1955 defense budget was another matter. After some deliberation, the Joint Chiefs of Staff (JCS) decided that no substantial changes could be made in the defense budget, which stood at $42 billion. The major reasons for this decision were that there was no change in the perceived threat, no change in the commitments to allies, and no new guidelines on the employment of nuclear weapons.[49]

Defense Secretary Charles Wilson presented this problem to the NSC at a meeting on October 13, 1953.[50] The reaction of Treasury Secretary George Humphrey, who expected a defense budget of $36 billion, and of Budget Director Joseph M. Dodge was what one source called horrified. It fell to Joint Chiefs of Staff Chairman Radford to defend the Joint Chiefs' premises, and he centered his discussion on the nature of presidential guidance for employment of nuclear weapons. His message, which was to have very significant results, was that if nuclear weapons would be used from the outset of a conflict, then a less costly force structure could be developed.

This led to a subsequent NSC session on October 30, at which the president approved NSC-162/2, the policy basis of the New Look.[51] This paper was based on Radford's suggestion of October 13, placing maximum reliance on nuclear weapons from the outset of a conflict. Radford's talk of October 13 had been entirely his own; neither the army nor the navy agreed with the new NSC policy on nuclear war. Nevertheless, Wilson, with Radford's help, was able to get qualified agreement on the new policy from Ridgway and Carney. Wilson and Radford now had a policy basis from which to pressure the army and navy to bring their force and budgetary estimates into line.

The immediate administrative problem then became one of developing the fiscal year 1955 defense budget so as to secure presidential approval by mid-December. Simultaneously, efforts were under way to develop the New Look from a concept into a specific JCS paper which would include projected force levels for fiscal years 1955, 1956, and 1957. By 1957 the New Look was to be fully implemented, barring some change in the overall situation that would require a new appraisal. Except at the top level, the development of the two documents followed separate paths. The budget followed its normal administrative channels from the services up to the secretary of defense. The New Look paper was prepared by a special JSC group. The two merged together at times because the fiscal year 1955 force goals were common to both. The budget, however, was the pacing factor, since it had to be completed by mid-December—so, therefore, did the New Look paper.

By early December an agreement of sorts had been reached within the Joint Chiefs of Staff on the New Look paper. Ridgway and Carney had predicated their agreement on a list of assumptions concerning the overall situation. Testifying in 1956, Ridgway, by then in a retired status, summarized the assumptions as follows: "These were in essence that there would be no substantial deterioration in the world situation, as well as a whole lot of others relating to Western Europe, Korea, and the Far East, and the growth of the Japanese force." [52] The significance of the assumptions was that Ridgway's concurrence in the New Look paper was conditional on their long-term validity. In any case, in December, Eisenhower approved both the New Look paper and the fiscal year 1955 defense budget. After almost a year in office, the president was ready to take his new strategic policy to the public and to Congress.

Throughout the late fall and winter of 1953–1954, high level administration spokesmen were engaged in the task of selling the New Look to the public. Some of the least dramatic efforts were made by Wilson himself around mid-November, before the preliminary work was completed. Speaking before the National Press Club on November 10, 1953, Wilson indicated that current planning might bring an end to the notion of balanced forces and place greater emphasis on air power, while reducing expenditures.[53] Not all members of the administration were speaking the same way, however. Any reader continuing down the *New York Times* column past the Wilson speech would find the following report of a speech by Ridgway in Cleveland the previous day: "General Matthew B. Ridgway said today the foot soldier still was the dominant factor in war and any weakening of U.S. ground forces now could be a grievous blow to freedom."

By December the speeches began to get more specific. On December 14 Admiral Radford addressed the National Press Club in Washington on the New Look. "A New Look is a resassessment of our strategic and logistic capabilities in the light of foreseeable developments, certain technological advances, the world situation today, and considerable estimating of future trends and developments. It is a searching review of this nation's military requirements for security. Thus our military task is complicated by the two requirements imposed upon us. We must be ready for tremendous vast retaliatory and counter-offensive blows in event of a global war and we must also be ready for lesser military action short of all-out war."[54]

The president's primary public pronouncements on the New Look came in his messages to Congress, specifically, the State of the Union message delivered on January 7, 1954, the annual budget message of January 21, and the annual message transmitting the Economic Report to the Congress on January 28.[55]

Of all the speeches made to explain the new defense policies, however, only that made by John Foster Dulles would be long remembered. His speech before the members and guests of the Council on Foreign Relations on January 12, 1954, was surely one of the great moments in the rhetoric of the cold war. The title of the speech was "Evolution of Foreign Policy." The speech was concerned not only with foreign policy but also with an explanation of, and the rationale for, the New Look strategic innovation. The speech was, said Dulles, an overall view of those foreign policies "which relate to our security."

The main part of the speech was entitled "Collective Security," in which the new policy was explained as follows:

We want, for ourselves and the other free nations, a maximum deterrent at a bearable cost.

Local defenses must be reinforced by the further deterrent of massive retaliatory power.

The way to deter aggression is for a free community to be willing and able to respond vigorously and at places and with means of its own choosing.

The basic decision was [made] to depend primarily on a great capacity to retaliate, instantly, by means and at places of our choosing.[56]

National and international reaction to the speech was intense and continued throughout the spring. Radford felt that the emphasis should have been on deterrence rather than on giving the impression "we were just ready to pounce on everybody." George Humphrey, though, had no doubts about massive retaliation: "That was what kept peace in the world. That and that alone, I am sure is what kept peace in the world. And all the rest of these soldiers and sailors and submariners and everything else, comparatively speaking, you could drop in the ocean, and it wouldn't make too much difference."[57]

Of the service chiefs, Twining alone was not skeptical. He felt that at the time the massive retaliation speech as an interpretation of the New Look was the "answer." He felt, in particular, that it was a stabilizing influence on a young NATO organization and increased our credibility as leader of the alliance. The speech subsequently developed such a life of its own that one tends to forget that Dulles was merely trying to explain the new Eisenhower defense policy in the overall context of foreign policy. Obviously, the intended audience went well beyond the immediate forum of the council. Perhaps this accounts for its oversimplification of the issues. Dulles's policy planning chief in those days, Robert Bowie, believes this to be the case.[58]

Quite obviously, the speech contained ambiguities. How did massive retaliatory power relate to local defense? What was meant by instant retaliation? These and other issues raised questions about the new policy that would take several months to clarify. What the speech did bring out was the involved relationships among foreign policy, military policy, and domestic economic policy. The New Look was an attempt to straddle all three. This major attempt to explain policy opened up more questions than it answered. In any case, the basis for the debate that was to follow had been established. The administration had its strategic policy and had made its public case; it was now time to make its case with Congress in connection with the fiscal year 1955 defense budget.[59]

As the president saw it, there were three factors that conditioned the administration's approach to Congress: the slimness of the Republican majority (eleven in the House and one in the Senate), unfamiliarity of Republicans with the technique of working with a president from their own party, and the wide variety of political outlooks among the Republican congressmen.[60]

Sherman Adams puts this in a somewhat different context: "The influential Republicans in Congress were, for the most part, conservatives who did nothing to help Eisenhower get the nomination nor did they accept the fact that he virtually saved their party from a deepening oblivion. They gave him only intermittent support and considerable opposition and personal aggravation. The Republican majority in Congress was so small during the first two years of the Eisenhower Administration that the President had to seek Democratic backing for his legislative programs and this added more strain on his relationship with the right wing of his own party." [61]

As a result, Eisenhower sought to bring the Congress around to his point of view by personal persuasion and compromise. The leadership of the Congress was exercised through the party organization on the Hill and not directly by the president. Eisenhower later set forth his rationale for avoiding a strong leadership role of the Eighty-third Congress in his memoirs, as follows: "The parties were so evenly balanced that we needed the vote of every one of our Republican Senators to put through the legislation in which we believed. . . . To obtain desirable legislation not only required us to keep the backing of most Republicans, but also often to win Democratic votes; so we had ceaselessly to explain, persuade, cultivate the understanding and confidence that go with personal friendship, and even cajole senators and representatives." [62]

There is a broader aspect of the president's perception of his role in relation to Congress, on which many writers have commented. That was his strong notion of the separateness of the two branches of government. According to Hughes, it was Eisenhower's feeling that Roosevelt had usurped powers of the legislature, which for two decades had been deprived of its proper role. [63]

In February 1954 the House Subcommittee on Defense Appropriations held hearings for the fiscal year 1955 defense budget, with Charles E. Wilson as the first witness. Wilson stressed that the New Look was a natural evolution from the hasty programming that had characterized Korean War planning. He further said that the fiscal year 1955 defense budget itself was based on the longer range New Look plan, which had been unanimously agreed upon by the Joint Chiefs of Staff. The economics that it offered were based on exploiting the capabilities of modern airpower. The program contemplated decreasing the active army by three divisions to seventeen; a relatively modest reduction in the number of navy ships; an air force of 120 wings, eventually to be 137 wings, down somewhat from the previous goal of 143 wings, "to be attained as soon as practicable after fiscal year 1954"; and an increase in monies for continental air defense of $1 billion over the previous fiscal year. [64] Under the mild probing of Clarence Cannon of Missouri, Wilson made two points that could be construed as indicating he did not wish to become involved in defending force goals in depth.

Two or three divisions in being, more or less, is not going to be [*sic*] the balance of power in the world.
I think we are also fortunate in having a President who understands military matters so thoroughly. [65]

The only serious probing Wilson received was from Robert L. F. Sikes, a Florida Democrat, who was also a reserve general in the army. Sikes began his questioning with the observation that the new defense program resulted in a weakening of the United States' defense posture, and it was soon clear he was referring primarily to army force reductions. As the questioning proceeded, it was evident Sikes had done his homework, and Wilson frequently suggested that some of the questions Sikes was posing could best be left for Radford's testimony.

Unlike Wilson, Radford's opening statement was off the record, for reasons of security. He subsequently inserted in the record a statement comparing the new and old military programs. The statement bears a marked resemblance to Radford's December speech to the National Press Club. It stressed, among other matters, the need for readiness, not only at the retaliatory level but also at the level of military actions short of general war. Sikes's time for questioning Radford was not long, and he was only able to probe whether Radford felt army reductions were a calculated risk, which Radford did not.

To hear testimony of the service secretaries and chiefs, the subcommittee was further subdivided into panels for each service. Army Secretary Stevens's testimony pointedly stressed that the reduction to a seventeen-division army was based upon certain assumptions having to do mainly with the completion of planned actions on the part of our allies and not on any statement of the Communist threat.[66] Ridgway, who followed Stevens, stressed in his prepared statement that army commitments were not declining but that army strength was declining. Neither official's statement gave any direct indication of serious misgivings concerning the overall program. Sikes's questioning, especially of Ridgway, was again incisive, but not to the point where the proposed defense program was openly challenged.

Admiral Carney's testimony was less qualified about the New Look than Ridgway's. Late in his questioning period, however, he made the point that the New Look was predicated upon no deterioration in the international situation. Should the situation deteriorate, a new New Look would be needed.[67]

Air force testimony showed considerably more satisfaction with the fiscal year 1955 defense budget than the other services. The thrust of the questioning was that since the air force once had a long-range program of 143 wings, why was 137 wings now considered satisfactory? The essence of Secretary Talbott's answer was that the present program was more realistic, and the air force stood behind it.[68]

House floor debate on the fiscal year 1955 defense budget took place on April 28 and 29, 1954. There was very little questioning of the underlying premises or strategic implications of the New Look. Such as there was came as a result of the efforts of three Democrats, Mahon, Sikes, and Price, and again Sikes was the most incisive. Mahon, being the senior opposition member of the Defense Appropriations Subcommittee, was probably the most authentic spokesman for his party. His remarks, however, were more supportive of the administration's program than critical. He placed great confidence in the president, particularly in the military area, and concluded that the administration was doing its best to provide an adequate defense program.[69] This was hardly an indictment of the New Look by the opposition party leaders.

Sikes's critique was different—and the only one that came close to questioning the validity of the New Look budget. He began by emphasizing his lack of enthusiasm for the defense budget, and particularly that portion pertaining to the army. In a statement reflecting what was in essence to become the major critique of the New Look, Sikes stated: "In this struggle for atomic supremacy it may not be long until we have reached a plateau . . . in the field of atomic warfare so that each would be fearful of employing such weapons against the other because of the fear of retaliation directed at their homeland. . . . We may be reaching the point where no one will dare pull the trigger. . . . It is much more likely we will continue to have brush fires like Korea."[70] The next speaker congratulated Sikes on his statesmanlike discussion, but he himself had a question on the air national guard program.

Price, on the concluding day of the debate, was also concerned with army effectiveness and the gamble that was being taken in the reduction in army strength. He spoke briefly, and no one

seemed to react much to his remarks.[71] Neither Sikes nor Price
carried his apprehensions about the defense program to the point
of offering any amendments to the appropriations bill. In the
end, the bill that passed was substantially what the administration had requested, although, in an economy mood of its own,
the House did make certain cuts in the administration's request.

Senate appropriation hearings were considerably shorter than
those in the House, with all matters of interest taking place on
the first two days. On the first day Senator Burnet R. Maybank,
a Democrat, inquired of Ridgway whether he was satisfied that
the army had sufficient funds.

A. I accept this decision as a sound one and am putting everything
we have behind its execution.

Q. I did not ask you if you accept it. . . . But do you recommend it?

A. The time for recommendation is past, sir.[72]

The probe was not pushed much further, with Ridgway suggesting an executive session as a better place for such discussion. Insofar as I can determine, the executive session never took place.

The following day, during the course of Radford's prepared
statement, he referred to unanimous agreement among the chiefs.
During brief questioning, Maybank wanted to know if all the
chiefs had really advocated the program, to which Radford replied "apparently not." Radford went on to explain that on
hearing the previous day's exchange with Maybank, he had concluded Ridgway was not satisfied with the program. As the discussion progressed Radford described the basic difference between
Ridgway and himself: "The difference comes as to whether we
agreed to accept the fact that the national economy over the long
pull is a military factor, and therefore the Chiefs would get estimates of the national income and make an assumption as to the
amount that might be allotted for defense." [73]

That really was the question, or at least one of them, in Ridgway's mind. Writing later, after his retirement, Ridgway made
clear that, except in a gross sense, consideration of economic fac-

tors constituted a dilution of professional military judgment. He further wrote that to compromise his judgment for other than convincing military reasons would destroy his usefulness as a professional military officer.[74]

There was one other hearing in the Senate at about the same time that is pertinent. This was the appearance of John Foster Dulles before the Committee on Foreign Relations, which was inquiring into the relationship between the defense program and foreign policy. In effect, this was an attempt to clarify the debate which Dulles had initiated in January with his speech to the Council on Foreign Affairs and which by spring was at its peak. In his testimony Dulles placed great emphasis on economic considerations. His explanation was a tribute to the efforts of George Humphrey: "If you put all your strength into a military establishment so that your own economy begins to decline, you are unable to be a vigorous economic center of the world which will help to sustain the viable economies in other countries, that could be just as disastrous as not having any military establishment at all."[75]

According to Dulles, the new policy clearly provided political guidance to the military to emphasize air and naval power and to deemphasize land power. He also made it clear that he viewed nuclear power as only one manner of retaliation. He declined, however, to become involved in any discussion of service strengths or the composition of the strategic reserve. Toward the end of the hearing a question from Democratic Senator Mike Mansfield led to a discussion of an important aspect of policy development. Having led Dulles into pronouncing the Eisenhower policy a new one, Mansfield sprang his trap. Since the policy was a new one, did not Dulles think that the proper committees of Congress, that is, the Armed Services Committee as well as those on Foreign Relations and Foreign Affairs, should have been consulted beforehand? Dulles's initial reaction, after considerable rambling, was that the presentation of the defense budget was the time for this consultation and this is the way it had been done. Mansfield disagreed and pointed out that policy matters were first in the purview of legislative committees. Only after that were the appropriations committees involved in providing the means to augment policy. Then, in a rare lecture to the formidable John Foster Dulles, Mansfield added: "The result has been that since you have made your speech in New York we have had all kinds of experts telling us what the new policy meant, and they were just guessing in the dark, as the rest of us were. I therefore hope that in the future you will seriously consider, at least, seeing the ranking members . . . so that we can be brought in for an understanding of just what the administration contemplates doing." [76]

Floor debate in the Senate was considerably livelier than it had been in the House and offered greater challenge to the administration. Senator Homer Ferguson made a standard presentation of the defense appropriation bill, stressing the long-haul concept, the notion of collective defense, and the integration into the program of new weapons technology. Senator Albert Gore opened the challenge by reading from a portion of Ridgway's prepared statement.

Senator John Kennedy followed with what seemed at first a gimmick, but shortly gave evidence of being a preoccupation. Was it not a fact that the budget was prepared at a time when it was believed that French operations in Indochina were going to be successful, Kennedy wanted to know. Of course it was a fact, but Ferguson denied its relevance to the budget. Quickly Kennedy shifted to the loss of three army divisions and subsequently linked these to potential manpower requirements for Southeast Asia.[77] Gore added that the New Look had already been proved a failure in Indochina. Ferguson appealed to the knowledge of the president in the military area, as well as the Joint Chiefs of Staff and the civilian leadership in the Pentagon. The Democratic opposition repeatedly returned to Ridgway's testimony, and especially to his exchange with Maybank. Senator Mike Monroney suggested that Ridgway had been "muzzled." Senator Hubert Humphrey joined the debate and summed up his view of the New Look policy as follows: "I wish to emphasize that the world situation is changing day by day. It does not do any good to talk about mass [*sic*] retaliation. It does not do any good to talk about something going to happen which is not going to happen. We have had our bluff called two or three times in the last month."[78]

On the second day of the debate Kennedy offered an amendment to the appropriation bill, the intent of which was to retain the army's strength at a level that would support nineteen divisions, as contrasted to the administration's proposal of seventeen divisions. The presentation of his case, mainly by himself and Monroney, generated more heat than light and in the end was defeated.

The New Look had weathered the congressional phase.[79] A year and a half after taking office Eisenhower had his strategic policy. Congressional examination of the basic premises and strategic concepts of the new policy had been virtually nonexistent. The administration's image of unanimity had remained intact, except for Ridgway, and his defection had been more implied than actual. Congressional probing was not deep. The most open challenge, the debate on the Senate floor, was neither systematic nor informed. In the end it turned out to be merely an opposition tactic that failed even to embarrass the administration.

It might be added that no defense policy of the United States in the 1950s could be developed completely in isolation, and certainly not a strategic innovation of the scope of the New Look. The NATO alliance, which was then, as now, the major U.S. defense commitment, obviously would have to approve the new policy. This was accomplished at the December 1954 ministerial session, when the council approved MC 48. This document placed major reliance on atomic weapons for the defense of Western Europe.

In view of the fact that Soviet military capabilities were growing and not decreasing, some rationale had to be provided. Dulles made three main points to the council supportive of MC 48: it was financially impossible to maintain two strategies, atomic and nonatomic; only atomic weapons could provide a forward defense; therefore MC 48, which represented the advice of the military to the council, should be approved. Even for a U.S.-

controlled NATO, this was rather transparent. However, since the allies, like the United States, perceived that they needed economies, they accommodated. The international context was perceived in terms of Soviet intentions, not capabilities, military jargon to the contrary, notwithstanding.

One issue which the policy of increased reliance on atomic weapons made more salient was that of nuclear sharing in the alliance context. The Atomic Energy Act of 1946 had been designed to keep secure American knowledge in the field of atomic weapons. Recognizing that NATO acceptance of the new strategic concept which MC 48 made official would raise the issue of a more liberal nuclear-sharing policy with our allies, the Eisenhower administration requested Congress to amend the 1946 act. The result was the Atomic Energy Act of 1954 which liberalized security provisions in minor ways for purposes of training allies to employ atomic weapons. However, the weapons themselves as well as the warheads were to remain in U.S. custody.

To sum up, three of Eisenhower's major campaign promises in 1952 had been oriented toward domestic problems, but their implementation had a significant influence on U.S. strategic policy. These promises were to liquidate the Korean War, to balance the budget, and to reduce taxes. Liquidation of the war did result in a reduced budget. Additional reductions in the budget were obtained at the expense of land forces under the New Look strategy. As a result of those actions, the Eisenhower administration was able to reduce taxes a year after taking office.

In subsequent years President Eisenhower was determined that his conservative economic views continue to be reflected in the budget. The defense budget became the centerpiece of his efforts. A breakdown in executive consensus over the defense budget was especially to be avoided, leading as it might to public pressure on Congress for greater defense expenditures. Such an outcome would alter the entire Eisenhower program. How successful he was in retaining his New Look strategy, controlling the defense budget, and retaining an executive consensus on defense matters needs to be considered.

## CHAPTER TWO

# The New Look Challenged

THE NEW LOOK that Eisenhower had established as his defense policy in 1954 came under increasing attack by 1956. The challenges came from scholars, writers, the military bureaucracy, and some congressmen. The scholarly and journalistic criticisms were to be expected; the New Look was inadequate in its logic and fair game for students of military strategy. Critics within the military establishment and the few congressional critics focused on the defense budget, using a number of different arguments.

In the presidential election of 1956, Adlai Stevenson, again the Democratic candidate, was unable to mount a serious challenge to Eisenhower. On matters of foreign policy, Eisenhower's image was strong. The French and British attack on Egypt and the uprisings in Hungary and Poland dominated the news in the final part of the campaign, and as a result public attention was focused on international crises. It was a poor time to appeal to the public to change presidents. But Eisenhower's image was also strong on domestic issues. The relative prosperity of the first Eisenhower administration did much to eliminate the public's mental association of a Republican president with a depression, which up to then had been the Hoover legacy.[1] Eisenhower's disposition to accept, and in mild ways to extend, the social welfare policies of the New Deal and the Fair Deal also served to reduce the Democratic advantage on domestic issues.

It might seem remarkable that Eisenhower's defense policy did not become an election issue in the 1956 campaign. Samuel Huntington's explanation probably comes fairly close to the truth: after the Korean War, the Democrats could not appear to be a war party; therefore, instead of selecting as an issue Eisenhower's inadequate defense efforts, it would be better to use issues that dramatized the Democratic opposition to war.[2] For these reasons, abolition of the draft and ending of nuclear testing were selected as the defense issues by the Democrats. Eisenhower was able to counter both issues successfully.

The election itself was an overwhelming personal victory for Dwight Eisenhower—457 electoral votes for him, 73 for Stevenson. Despite this victory, the president was unable to carry either house in with him; this was the first time that had happened in over one hundred years. By 1956, however, Eisenhower was accustomed to working with a Congress controlled by Democrats, since the 1954 elections had taken away the small Republican majority.[3] The Eighty-fourth Congress and the administration had worked together quite harmoniously, and this ambience continued after the 1956 elections. The working relationships between the conservative president and the mildly liberal congressional leaders, Lyndon Johnson in the Senate and Sam Rayburn in the House, remained good until the latter part of 1959, when preliminary activities for the 1960 presidential election began.

The international context of U.S. defense policy was in flux in 1955–1956. Early 1955 was a period of debate among Soviet leaders in defense policy. Georgi Malenkov, who was removed from office in February, had argued for a cautious foreign policy and for the necessity of peaceful coexistence in light of nuclear capability on both sides. His opponents, led by Nikita Khrushchev and the new premier, Nikolai Bulganin, quickly took steps to increase the defense budget by some 12 percent.[4]

On Aviation Day, in July 1955, the new Soviet leaders held a flyby of their new Bison strategic aircraft and gave the impression that there had been large-scale production of the bomber. In fact, according to the director of the CIA, it was the same squadron of ten aircraft that circled overhead again and again.[5] Following this demonstration, estimates began to appear of a large Soviet lead in bombers by 1957. This estimate was based on Soviet capabilities, not intentions, which, as it later turned out, were to limit bomber production.

The Soviets were vague about delivery means, stressing instead their possession of nuclear weapons of mass destruction. In fact, 1955–1957 was a period in which Soviet leadership was giving priority to the development of missiles, not the production of bombers. But a proclivity on the part of certain American writers to believe the worst concerning the Soviet strategic capabilities helped develop the notion of a "bomber gap" beginning in 1955. The lesson of the "bomber gap" to the Soviet leaders was the obvious tendency of the West to exaggerate the strategic capabilities of the USSR. This was a lesson that was to be put to good use two years later in connection with their ICBM (Intercontinental Ballistic Missile) successes.[6]

In the fall of 1956, just before the presidential election, came the twin crises of Hungary and Suez. The failure of the United States to intervene in Hungary confirmed the general belief that the "liberation" pledge of the 1952 campaign was rhetoric. In terms of strategic policy, it also confirmed that the strategic superiority of the United States would be used only for defense of the West. In the Suez crisis, the Soviet hint of employing rockets on Britain and France influenced public opinion, especially in England and the Arab world.[7] These hints, however, had no effect on the strategic policy of the United States or NATO.

What did affect the NATO tactical nuclear weapons strategy was the progress made by the Soviet Union in equipping her forces with nuclear weapons. The result was a lessened confidence on the part of NATO officials that the West would have the advantage in fighting a nuclear war. Their skepticism did not, however, persuade these officials, or at least their governments, that

NATO's conventional capabilities should be built up. Rather, the conventional forces came to be regarded increasingly as a "trip wire" and the tactical nuclear weapons as a deterrent to aggression rather than a defense. In December 1956, at a meeting of the North Atlantic Council, the defense ministers of Britain, France, the Netherlands, and Turkey requested that tactical nuclear warheads, under control of the United States, be made available to European forces (other than German) to increase their value as a deterrent. Although Secretary Dulles promised the allies that the United States would accelerate allied training and speed up the development of warhead stockpiles in Europe, there was no change in the requirement for custody of the warheads by the United States. Said Dulles: "The United States is prepared, if this Council so wishes, to participate in a NATO atomic stockpile. Within this stockpile system, nuclear warheads would be deployed under United States custody in accordance with NATO defensive planning and in agreement with the nations directly concerned. In the event of hostilities, nuclear warheads would be released to the appropriate NATO Supreme Allied Commander for employment by nuclear-capable NATO forces."[8]

Important to the context of the strategic decisions in 1956 was the president's heart attack, suffered in September 1955 in Denver. Eisenhower remained in Fitzsimmons General Hospital for about six weeks, returning to Washington in November. Sherman Adams was sent to Denver to administer all government business coming to and from the president.

After Eisenhower's return to Washington, access to the president became more of a problem than it had been previously. Sherman Adams, who did have access, already enjoyed considerable latitude in domestic matters, such as no one enjoyed in foreign policy or defense issues. Dulles had access to the president and continued to check out his own views on major matters with Eisenhower. But there was no Dulles in the Pentagon, and in the period after the heart attack, access was not easy for either Secretary Wilson or Chairman Radford.

At the service chief level, this was for a time a significant problem. Maxwell Taylor (who succeeded Ridgway as army chief of staff in 1955) recalls that one of his major objectives, which the heart attack frustrated, was to establish a closer relationship between the army chief of staff and the president.[9] There was, however, one individual of lesser military rank who did have access— Brigadier General Andrew J. Goodpaster. Goodpaster was both staff secretary under Adams (subsequently under Persons) and defense liaison officer. In this latter role he was pretty much on his own. Eisenhower considered Goodpaster's work in national security affairs as more important than his other functions and viewed it as overlapping the role of the special assistant for national security affairs.

Until the summer of 1957 only two major officials concerned with defense left office: General Ridgway, army chief of staff, and Admiral Carney, chief of naval operations. Ridgway's position within the administration had become untenable by 1955 because of his opposition to the reduced role of the army under Eisenhower's strategy. The clear front runner for the Ridgway appointment was General Maxwell Davenport Taylor, then Far East commander. Taylor was an impressive-looking officer, smooth, and a good speaker, with the reputation of being something of an intellectual. He had risen in reputation within his service in the latter part of World War II, and, as these things sometimes happen, the conventional wisdom in the army seemed to point to his eventual appointment as chief of staff.

Before making the appointment, however, the commander-in-chief wanted to talk with Taylor. Since the army was the main problem for the president in attempting to maintain his strategic consensus in 1955, this was an important appointment. The president wanted certain assurances from Taylor before his appointment as chief of staff.[10] First, Taylor must "understand and wholeheartedly accept that his primary responsibility related to his joint duties." Second, he must hold views on strategic doctrine "which are in accord with those of the president." Since it would be necessary for the new army chief to express his opinion and convictions openly when called upon, such agreement in advance was essential. "Loyalty in spirit as well as in letter was necessary." Taylor indicated understanding and acceptance of the president's views.

When Taylor arrived in Washington in the summer of 1955 to assume his new duties, however, he brought with him a proposal for a new strategy that he called Flexible Response, which emphasized lower thresholds of war than envisioned in the New Look. He first introduced this strategy into the joint arena in March 1956 and placed himself in opposition to the JCS chairman, the air force chief, the secretary of defense, and the president. Radford had favored another army officer to be chief of staff and apparently experienced difficulties with Taylor, finding him hard to work with.[11] Another service chief said he found Taylor an enigma and difficult to get along with. Perhaps this is not surprising, considering the scope of what Taylor was trying to do.[12]

Robert Carney's tour as chief of naval operations lasted approximately the same two years as Ridgway's term as army chief of staff. His critique of the New Look had been considerably more muted than Ridgway's, but he had problems in his working relationships. One official close to the scene felt that Navy Secretary Thomas was the prime mover in Carney's departure.[13]

Unlike Taylor, Admiral Arleigh Burke's appointment to replace Carney apparently came as a genuine surprise. Burke was relatively junior, being still a two-star admiral when selected for chief of naval operations over ninety admirals senior to him. In his preappointment interviews in May 1955, both the secretary and undersecretary of the navy alluded to differences of opinion between Carney and themselves. Subsequently, Burke met with the secretary of defense and the president. Wilson treated him to a homily, the main point of which was the need for greater cooperation between the military and civilian leaders. The president stressed what many other similar appointees had heard: the need for teamwork once a decision had been made. His other points, also recurring ones, were the importance of JCS corporate activities and the desirability of delegating service responsibilities to the vice chiefs.[14]

The navy's strategic concept during the Eisenhower years fluctuated somewhere between those of the air force and the army. Eisenhower's stress on nuclear delivery allowed the naval aviators to consolidate their dominance in the navy by the time Burke became chief.[15] Subsequently, because of advances in nuclear propulsion and the solid-fueled Polaris missile, the submarine forces came into their own as part of the strategic deterrent. This latter development, in time, increased the navy's emphasis on the effectiveness of carrier aircraft in limited-war situations.

I would like to turn now to that rather remarkable group of critiques and commentaries concerning the Eisenhower strategic innovation which flourished in the mid- and late-1950s. John Foster Dulles's speech of January 12, 1954, was the catalyst for the great debate of the 1950s over U.S. defense policy. By the fall of that year, the immediate flurry of criticism and clarification of the administration's policy was over. There followed, over a period of many years, a rather large volume of scholarly and journalistic analyses and writings on U.S. defense policy. These writers went beyond merely faulting the administration's policy of massive retaliation, as it had come to be known from Dulles's speech, and set forth various alternative policies. Some writers concentrated on alternative deterrence strategies, but the majority focused on various notions of limited war.

Proponents of limited war sought to make nuclear deterrence more credible by filling in what they perceived to be gaps in the ladder of escalation. It was incredible, they theorized, to react to local aggression with nuclear weapons. One of the questions raised was what size military force was required below the nuclear threshold; obviously Eisenhower felt he had a large enough force, while his opponents felt the opposite. Within the bureaucracy, the army encouraged the limited-war challenge, which came largely from the academic world and which included just about every strategic writer of note.[16]

One of the first of such writers was Bernard Brodie, writing in November 1954, who set forth the need for a limited-war policy in order to avoid total war. What may well have been the classic critique of the massive retaliation policy was William W. Kaufmann's "The Requirements of Deterrence." Kaufmann pointed out that the Eisenhower policy assumed central control of the Communist world by Moscow and Peking, cost-risk calculations on the part of the Communist leaders roughly the same as for those of the United States, and the ability to forestall action by the Communist powers along their periphery by posing to their leaders costs and risks greater than their potential gains.[17]

The practicability of the Eisenhower policy, Kaufmann said, depended on the answers to two questions: what were the requirements for an effective deterrence policy, and did the objective conditions permit fulfillment of these requirements? The basic requirement, he said, was a policy credible to the enemy, to allies, and to the domestic audience. Credibility in turn involved capability, cost advantage, and intentions. If the capability is assumed, making intentions credible is an extremely difficult problem; to make a policy credible, it must be based on domestic and allied support, as well as some reasonable relationship between the objective desired and the costs involved. Did the objective situation permit meeting these requirements for a policy of massive retaliation? Kaufmann concluded that the minimum requirements for credibility were not met. He based this conclusion on the U.S. record in the international arena and on the state of allied and domestic opinion. He said the policy might well be credible for contingencies involving the vital interests of the United States. But there was a vast number of actions open to the Communist leaders that did not affect interests vital to the United States and for which more credible alternative policies must, he concluded, be devised. Kaufmann suggested that these must include willingness to employ conventional power on the periphery of the Communist world. As far as U.S. capabilities were concerned, he pointed out the need for strengthening ground and tactical air forces, but not at the expense of strategic forces.

The British, who had in fact adopted a nuclear-heavy strategy emphasizing nuclear power before the United States did, were also in on the debate. P. M. S. Blackett, writing in 1956, stated: "I see the problem not as how many atomic bombs we can afford but as how few we need. For every hundred million pounds spent for . . . preparations for global war, which almost certainly will not happen, is so much less for limited and colonial wars, which well may." Another British theorist, Rear-Admiral Sir Anthony Buzzard, stressed the value of tactical nuclear weapons. He was not without opponents, including Blackett, who subsequently criticized the notion of nuclear limited war as being destabilizing.[18]

In 1957 writings were published in the United States which had a major impact in focusing the debate on the theory of limited war. The most widely read of these was a best seller, Henry Kissinger's *Nuclear Weapons and Foreign Policy*.[19] The central point of Kissinger's attack was the proposition, put forth by administration spokesmen, that if the United States had sufficient military power for a major war, it had enough for any threat of lesser magnitude. His thesis was that U.S. emphasis on strategic power had made it vulnerable to lesser challenges, for which nuclear retaliation, in effect global war, was not an appropriate response. Strategic warfare had limited ability to influence an opponent in cases where the stakes were so small that massive retaliation would not seem a credible response. He agreed that strategic forces had their place, but so did a limited-war capability. The two were, in fact, complementary.

There were three aspects of Kissinger's work that received particular criticism: his belief that numbers of soldiers do not count on a tactical nuclear battlefield; his heavy reliance on technological innovations not yet achieved (for instance, a substitute for the internal combustion engine); and his belief that Western soldiers would be much more capable than Soviet soldiers on an atomic battlefield, because of their greater initiative and self-reliance.

The most extensive, and perhaps most critical, review of Kissinger's book was by William W. Kaufmann.[20] Kissinger's doctrine, Kaufmann felt, had been developed without regard to such realities as technological feasibility and resources likely to be made available to the military establishment. Since Kissinger had ignored these basic calculations, he had simply sketched out a possible course of action and had not demonstrated that it was preferable to other alternatives. Further, the tactical nuclear alternative he did develop was based upon "the fantasy of self-sufficient mobile units; ignoring the air battle; and minimizing the effects of nuclear weapons." The result, Kaufmann felt, was that Kissinger's effort was special pleading rather than a systematic analysis.

The Kissinger book, notwithstanding the criticism of it, was generally well received by opponents of massive retaliation. Although it was the best-known book on this subject at the time, there was another of equally high quality published slightly earlier by Robert Osgood.[21] Osgood's discussion of the employment of nuclear weapons in limited war was more balanced than Kissinger's, although, like Kissinger, he concluded that such weapons should be used. Osgood did not, however, develop a model of warfare, as Kissinger had done, and it was only in his final chapter that he set forth his proposed limited-war strategy. His thesis was set forth rather tentatively because he was concerned about the unanswered questions concerning the employment of tactical nuclear weapons. Could such a war be limited? Does it really permit economy in ground forces? How does such warfare meet cases of overt aggression? These and other unanswered questions posed by Osgood mirrored an air of uncertainty on the part of many persons about tactical nuclear warfare, which was to continue well past the Eisenhower administration.

The launching of the Soviet satellite Sputnik in October 1957 changed the emphasis of those writing on strategic matters. Many writers became aware that the technological potential of the Soviet Union made that nation not only a threat but also a partner of sorts, if stable deterrence were to be achieved.[22] Three of the better-known strategic thinkers writing in the post-Sputnik period were Albert Wohlstetter, Oskar Morgenstern, and Bernard Brodie.

Wohlstetter set forth his views in *Foreign Affairs* in early 1958.[23] The requirements to maintain a stable balance, he pointed out, were both complex and expensive and involved the ability to survive enemy attacks, to communicate the decision to retaliate, and to penetrate enemy defenses and reach the selected targets. What was required, in short, was an invulnerable retaliatory force.

Morgenstern, writing in 1959, suggested that greatest stability could be obtained if both the United States and the USSR developed seaborne missiles, which would be invulnerable. Finally, in 1959, Bernard Brodie published his *Strategy in the Missile Age*, which tied together the strategic thinking that had been set forth during the period of ferment since 1954. The requirements as he saw them were an invulnerable strategic retaliatory force and an ability to cope with local conflict without resort to nuclear weapons.[24]

These writings were all attempting to set forth rational solutions to what appeared to be the logical inadequacies of the New Look. They were not arguing against the containment policies of the Eisenhower administration, nor were they suggesting any form of détente with the Soviet Union.[25] They were, however, rejecting—usually implicitly—the Eisenhower thesis that the U.S. economy could not stand the expenditures necessary for conventional forces of the size many of these writers envisioned.

While these writings served as a useful theoretical basis for the United States Army and sometimes the United States Navy positions, there is no evidence that the White House paid much attention to them. It is true that in September 1957 Dulles published an article in *Foreign Affairs* which stressed the importance of local defense with tactical nuclear weapons, but defense budgets were not increased to improve limited-war forces. The great defense debate of the 1950s was intellectually vigorous but politically futile until 1961.

In his budget message of January 16, 1956, the president presented very little that was new in the defense field except for a proposed increase in missile procurement. The message restated the basic principles of the New Look: a long-haul posture with emphasis on retaliatory capability and continental defense; maximum use of science and technology to minimize manpower requirements; and a buildup of ready reserves at the expense of active land forces, because of the difficulties in deploying the latter immediately upon the outbreak of hostilities. The president envisioned a total defense budget of about $35.5 billion.[26]

Pressures on the administration to raise the level of its defense expenditures soon developed in Congress. These were not related to any extraordinary external event, but mainly to the fact that 1956 was a presidential election year. It was impossible in early 1956 to challenge the president on war and peace issues or economic conditions. Therefore, in the defense area the opposition concentrated on Eisenhower's obsession with cutting defense budgets and on his alleged lack of sufficient emphasis on missile development. As the months went by, however, pressures came not only from Congress but also from air force efforts to secure additional funds for the strategic bomber force. To a lesser extent, the army and navy were also pressuring for more funds. At this point it would be useful in order to understand these conflicting views, to examine each of the service positions of that time, particularly at their point of greatest emphasis, the issue of modernizing the forces.

Although by now the army had become the chief sponsor of the limited-war concept, army leaders also saw their service as having a place in other strategic plans. Specifically, they viewed the army as part of the overall deterrent and as part of the balanced force they felt would be required in event of a general war. To fill these three roles the army would have to develop new types of combat organization and new weaponry. For example, developments in atomic weapons research made possible the selective use of atomic weapons by ground forces. This in turn required the development of suitable delivery systems, as well as tactical organizations capable of fighting in a battlefield situation where such weapons were being employed by both sides.

The problem was further complicated because the army leaders thought they should be able to fight both conventional and nuclear wars. The total requirement, as they viewed it, was new weapons systems, new types of combat organizations, new means of transportation, advanced communications, a better tactical intelligence system, and more effective supply techniques.[27] In the opinion of the army leaders, these requirements were not met in the defense budget for fiscal 1957 as approved by the president.

By early 1956, the navy had not yet joined the army in its open enthusiasm for limited war. The carrier, which was the navy's prime ship, however, was viewed as usable in both limited and general war situations. And Chief of Naval Operations Arleigh Burke declared that antisubmarine warfare was being given the highest navy priority. The navy's long-range missile, the Polaris, was not yet a reality, but it was an active program from the time Admiral Burke became CNO in August 1955. Burke summed up the navy modernization program in 1956 as follows: "We are going from props to jets, from oil burners to nuclear reactors, from subsonic to supersonic, from TNT to nuclear warheads, from conventional shells to missiles, from atmosphere to space." Unlike the army, the navy received funds adequate for their modernization program in the fiscal year 1957 defense budget.[28]

The air force's modernization requirements caused the greatest pressure on the administration in the spring of 1956. In particular, the strategic bomber force became the focus of attention within the administration and in Congress. The air force position on the question of missiles or bombers in the mid-1950s was that ultimately the ICBM would be the major weapon but that manned bombers would remain the primary weapon for a long time. In the spring of 1955 American intelligence, and subsequently air force officials and others, overreacted to a USSR demonstration of advanced aircraft. The immediate concern was that these aircraft had become operational considerably earlier than intelligence officials had predicted. Since the size and composition of the United States Strategic Air Command (SAC) had been based on a different scenario, there began an intense reassessment of SAC capabilities.

In 1955 and 1956 there were numerous articles in the press stressing Soviet progress in both bombers and missiles.[29] During the same period an assistant secretary of the air force for research and development, Trevor Gardner, suddenly resigned. He cited as his reason the failure of the administration to remove budgetary restrictions on force modernization, in particular missile development. It was in this atmosphere that Senator Stuart Symington, a former air force secretary, proposed that air power hearings be held by his subcommittee of the Senate Armed Services Committee. These hearings, held from April until July 1956, put considerable pressure on the administration, although the report of the hearings was not published until after Eisenhower's second inauguration in January 1957.

Not unmindful of service competition for the available defense dollars, the president had the chairman and chiefs come over to the White House in early February 1956 so that he could give them a little advice. Eisenhower "felt that great harm had been done in the past" when the chiefs gave out individual service views "without regard to announced administration policy." He realized that they were under great pressure from their subordinates, but they should act as a corporate body and shape individual service views "into the larger purpose."[30]

A few days later he met with Radford and the subject of local war came up.[31] He said he was "not going to permit small packets of troops all around the [Eurasian] periphery." Further, "in local wars . . . he felt sure we would use tactical atomic weapons" if required. "There might," he added, "be other situations where political effects might be overriding and preclude such use at least at the outset."

By March 1956 pressures on the administration, coupled with prodding by the House Appropriations Committee, caused the president to consider requesting supplemental appropriations to accelerate modernization. The chiefs, after looking into their requirements, proposed raising the defense budget goal developed in 1953 by four to six billion dollars annually. Wilson and Radford brought a draft memorandum representing the chiefs' thinking to the president's office on the afternoon of March 13. The president thought the document portrayed a "very dark picture." He did not agree with the impression given by the memorandum that the U.S. military position had worsened in the last several years. The president went on to say that to him "there seemed to be a premise that we are the only ones resisting communism, and that if we are to have allies we must practically pay for their efforts." He thought it might be better "to encourage some nations to be neutral." There was, he thought, too much of an inclination to ask for all defense that might be desirable. The point was to judge where to take the risks. The problem was to analyze where the best return in security for the dollar could be obtained. The president wanted Wilson to have each chief take the same view toward the importance of a sound economy as did Radford.[32]

Subsequently, on March 29 the Defense Department forwarded to the White House a trimmed-down supplemental request totaling over one-half billion dollars, of which the largest portion was for air force modernization, mainly increased bomber production. The following day the chiefs met with the president in his office. One of the areas of discussion concerned modernization of the forces.[33] Radford indicated there were numerous issues that needed resolution, including the roles and missions of the services in relation to missiles. There was also a desire by the army to control its own aerial reconnaissance. The president felt that Wilson should put plenary powers in the hands of one man in the missile field and that that individual should make the decisions in regard to missiles. The discussion on army matters was deferred until a meeting Maxwell Taylor was to have with the president in a few days.

Eisenhower then moved on to discuss what was really on his mind. "It was in the nature of our government," he felt, "that everyone except for a few people at top were working to damage the economy," because they perceived their own agency as needing more resources to improve its operation. In addition, in the case of military expenditures, there were great pressures from the press and from Congress that were not helpful. In working for permanent security, he felt that there must be a sensitivity toward keeping the economy viable and strong. He did not expect the chiefs to abandon their convictions toward security needs, but he did expect service activities to be on "a spartan basis, and with awareness of the essentiality of a sound economy to true security."

On April 3 the president met in his office with George Humphrey, Budget Director Percival F. Brundage (Eisenhower's third budget director), and others to make a decision on the proposed supplemental appropriation.[34] The president felt it was unlikely that defense expenditures could be brought below the present levels. Humphrey recommended that the president approve the supplemental request as proposed by the defense department, but felt a thorough review of U.S. security commitments around the world was definitely needed.

On the same day, the president met with General Taylor on army force modernization. Taylor outlined his views on army aviation and missiles; he felt there should be no artificial constraints based on weights or ranges of aircraft, but rather, that the army should be permitted to develop what they would best use in their operations. The president wondered what use the army would have for the 1,500-mile missile that it had under development. Taylor indicated that the army wanted to keep the question open, but in the meantime was taking advantage of its expertise to develop such a missile. The main concern of the president was that the army was taking on missions through lack of confidence that the air force would meet the army's needs. Basically, he opposed this approach and felt that each service should insist on the others' providing the required support.

On April 5 the president met in his office with Humphrey, Wilson, Brundage, and Radford to complete action on the supplemental request for fiscal year 1957. He said that his great concern with the proposal, which he had approved, was that it would "lay groundwork for a permanently higher program in future years."[35] He pointed out that it was the secretary of the treasury who had finally persuaded him to approve the supplemental. Now that this had been done, everyone should be careful not to be led into statements in Congress or elsewhere supporting a particular service at the expense of the Defense Department as a whole. Eisenhower felt that anyone of high position who would not rise above the partisan outlook of a particular service "did not belong in the position he holds." He said that everyone in the administration testifying before Congress should support the supplemental as approved by him. Wilson felt the supplemental was adequate and would be disappointed if all the top people did not accept it on that basis. Wilson also indicated that it might be a good idea to develop three-year defense programs in the future. Humphrey said that the current action related to fiscal year 1957, and in time he would have some very definite ideas on fiscal year 1958 and later defense budgets.

The president then commented on reports he had been receiving from Congress that interservice tensions were worsening. He saw no reason for such a situation. He wanted the chiefs to stick to presenting corporate opinion when going before Congress. Single "service opinions and points of view were of no value" to him. If the administration talked in a unified way there would be no basis for anyone's being alarmed. The present appropriations hearings seemed, to him, to be concentrating on getting each service chief to say he needed more than was provided in the budget. If a chief could not bring himself to support the administration's strategy and defense budget, then he did not belong in the position he held.

Later in the month, in a meeting with Radford, Eisenhower referred to a recent air force press release about a plane that could reach speeds of 1,500 miles per hour.[36] As part of the service competition in those days, each service liked to publicize equipment in the blueprint stage, as an aid in securing development funds for the project. He had, he told Radford, called Air Force Secretary Donald Quarles to ask why it was necessary to have such a big spread in the newspapers on that item. He stressed to Quarles the need to avoid this type of article which results only in increased interservice competitive publicity.

There was another publication that was bothering the president that spring. Ridgway's memoirs had appeared first in the *Saturday Evening Post* and then in book form.[37] Ridgway was highly critical of Eisenhower's strategic policy. In a meeting with Radford in May, the president indicated he had been considering how best to handle this type of problem.[38] He was thinking of asking for "a new kind of oath, to be taken by all military and civilian officials who served in the Pentagon." The oath would be such that, on termination of an individual's tour of duty, he could "disclose nothing that the department of defense determined was security information." In addition, the president said he was considering stricter rules with regard to statements concerning government policy by officers who were already retired.

Other meetings were held that spring in the president's office, which, while not relating directly to the fiscal 1957 defense budget, would influence future budgets. These concerned the Joint Strategic Objectives Plan (JSOP), a document that in theory was the source of guidance for the military on future defense budgets.

In late March, in a meeting at which the chiefs had the JSOP on their minds, Chairman Radford raised an important question. There was, Radford brought out, a "reluctance in some quarters" to plan on the use of atomic weapons. He himself felt already committed to their use, based on current and projected force structures. The president indicated that while this was a subject requiring great care in discussion, he felt that "in any war involving the Soviet we would use atomics." In mid-May Radford again met with the president and said that in JSOP discussions in the Pentagon the question had again arisen whether atomic weapons would be used in small wars.[39] The president was inclined to believe we should "not get involved" in small conventional wars, that is, "beyond the size of several U.S. battalions. Anything of Korean proportions," for example, "would become one for the use of atomics." The president felt that American participation in small wars was primarily a matter for naval and air units. In the same meeting Radford expressed the opinion that in the event of engagement in Vietnam, the army's task would be mainly to provide advisory personnel. The other army tasks, he believed, would be to provide Honest John (an atomic weapon) and other missile units as support to indigenous forces.

In late May another meeting, consisting of Eisenhower, Radford, and Taylor, was held on the JSOP. The issue turned on the definition of general war.[40] Taylor pointed out that the air force, navy, and the chairman of the Joint Chiefs of Staff were of the opinion that all planning should be based on the use of atomic weapons. By 1960 he predicted both sides would reach a situation of nuclear deterrence, which caused him to believe that any war was likely to be a small one. Two differences of view had developed, Taylor pointed out to the president. He alone among the Joint Chiefs felt that general war should be defined in such a way that limitations on the use of atomic weapons should be recognized as a possibility. (This strategic argument, translated into resource terminology, had a direct bearing on the size of the land force establishment that was required.) The others felt that in a general war involving the United States and the USSR, atomic weapons would be used from the outset. The other difference concerned the use of atomic weapons in conditions short of general war. Taylor felt that conventional forces gave much more flexibility in small war situations, and we ought not to plan so definitely to use atomic weapons in such conflicts.

The president thought it was "fatuous" to think that a conflict between the United States and the USSR could take place without atomic weapons being employed. Although he agreed that the term "massive retaliation" had been ridiculed, he felt that it would be the key to survival in a war with the Soviets. As for local wars, the main support to indigenous forces would be U.S. air and naval forces, with only light U.S. land forces, and then only at critical points. He would use "the most efficient weapons" available, and since tactical atomic weapons were now practically integral to U.S. forces, the Joint Chiefs should plan on their use in small wars.

Taylor then outlined his notions of a finite deterrence strategy. By this Taylor meant nuclear sufficiency covering multiple contingencies, but avoiding an atomic war-fighting capability.

Taylor felt that if one proceeds on to requirements for actually fighting atomic wars, these requirements become practically limitless. He felt that the proper priority was finite deterrence, flexible forces for small wars, and whatever resources were left could go toward fighting an all-out atomic war. The president acknowledged that the position he had previously outlined did not leave much for the army in the first year of a war. He felt, however, in a nuclear war the army would be mainly concerned with "establishing and maintaining order within the U.S." Radford interjected that the president's decision supported the majority view within the Joint Chiefs, and with that Taylor finally found something with which to agree.

As for the fiscal year 1957 defense budget itself, in the end the House joined the Senate in increasing air force funds by about $800 million above the president's total request, including his supplemental request. This was largely for accelerated aircraft procurement. Congress seemed to have little difficulty grasping SAC's request for modernization. On the other hand, army modernization made little impression on the Eighty-fourth Congress, and the army received $200 million less than the president had requested. The navy budget went quietly through Congress with a loss of only $50 million.

The supplemental appropriations then came about as a result of pressures from the Congress, the press, and the air force. The primary issue was the need to accelerate force modernization. The entire episode of the fiscal year 1957 supplemental appropriations seems to show that the budget was Eisenhower's primary device to shape strategic policy. This differs from the accepted textbook notion that the defense budget was developed to support a strategic policy developed in the National Security Council. Eisenhower obviously felt that existing forces were adequate for deterrence, for limited war if it came, or for general war in such an eventuality. The perceptions of the service chiefs were in differing ways and degrees opposed to Eisenhower's, partly because they did not hold his view that increased budgets were a threat to the economy and, therefore, ultimately to the security of the country.

Late in the spring of 1956, Secretary Wilson did initiate a three-year look at defense requirements, an idea he had brought up at a meeting with the president in April. The outcome of the study was a goal of "sufficient deterrence," actually a modification of the New Look. It was articulated by Donald Quarles, then deputy defense secretary, in August 1956 and was based upon the growing nuclear capability of the USSR. As Quarles set it forth, deterrence rested not so much on the relative strategic strength of both sides as on their absolute ability to inflict unacceptable damage to each other.[41]

Another outcome of the three-year look was a defense budget ceiling of $38 billion. But when Wilson called for preliminary estimates of the fiscal year 1958 defense budget, the outcome was a whopping $48.5 billion. It was evident something was going to have to give, and Radford thought he had the answer. In discussing the JSOP with the president in May, the possibility of any sizable war without nuclear weapons had been ruled out. On this basis, Radford led a major effort to reduce military manpower by 800,000 men, leaving a total force of two million. In his plan, major reductions would come from the army and would have reduced that service's deployments in Europe and Asia to small atomic task forces.[42] The plan was leaked and appeared in an article by Anthony Leviero in the *New York Times* of July 13, 1956. The furor, especially in Germany, was such that the plan was quickly dropped.

In late July there was a meeting in the president's office concerning the budget. Wilfred McNeil, the defense comptroller, presented an overview based upon the estimates that by now had gained support within the bureaucracy.[43] The president felt it was a mistake to have allowed the preliminary estimate of $48.5 billion to be given any status. Wilson, no doubt under Radford's influence, felt the best way to reduce the figure was by reducing manpower. The president disagreed; he felt that every program must be scrutinized for possible reduction. He was disappointed that the service chiefs could not "rise above the service approach" to national security. "It is," he said, "necessary for the civilians to exercise leadership and control over the military to bring about budget reductions." Wilson thought it was going to be difficult to get down to the goal of $38 billion without drastically upsetting current programs.

These high figures represented the rapid technological changes that the services were embracing in their force modernization programs. By the summer of 1956, the army had decided to undertake the atomic approach with zeal. Under the rubric of PENTANA (pentagonal atomic-nonatomic army), the army developed something called the Pentomic Division. This was a small division, designed to fight in either an atomic or conventional war. The unit had five battle groups (hence, the appellation pentomic) and an atomic capability, although the latter was primarily in the planning stage. Without changing their basic belief that the United States needed conventional capabilities, the army leaders felt that the psychology of something new and atomic would assist in this budget battle.

In October the army chief of staff, Maxwell Taylor, briefed the president on the new organization.[44] He stated the four principles that had been observed in developing the new organization: adapting the division to the atomic battlefield; pooling those units only needed occasionally; expanding the area of control by taking advantage of improved communications capabilities; and basing the organization on new equipment, some of which was yet to be developed. The last principle, in particular, was designed to establish the groundwork for future expansion in the army budget.

The president, though interested, seemed mainly concerned about the technique of handling publicity on the new organization. He felt that no stress should be given to the placing of atomic weapons in the new divisions. Wilson, concerned about manpower, wondered whether there would be any overall savings. The president felt that the incorporation of atomic firepower into the division would certainly allow overall personnel reductions. It was Taylor's and the army's view that a tactical nuclear battlefield required more, not fewer, people, but no one was listening.

The navy force modernization program planned for fiscal year 1958 was extensive, concentrating on three areas. First, there was the nuclear shipbuilding program, including a supercarrier to be propelled by nuclear energy. The value of the nuclear carrier over one conventionally powered was summed up by a later secretary of the navy, who described its characteristics as: "(1) being free operationally of the requirement for logistic fuel support—particularly in conflict, (2) ability to operate warships reliably over long periods of time at high sustained speeds and (3) the strategic and tactical gain of eliminating a major at-sea replenishment requirement." [45] The most extensive use of nuclear propulsion by the navy, however, was in its submarines, which began coming into the fleet in numbers in 1957.

The second area of concentration was the ship modernization program. This involved the improvement of existing ships or their replacement and the substitution of new weapons systems for old. The third area of concentration probably had the most far-reaching potential for the navy: the fleet ballistic-missile submarine, on which construction began in 1957. Shortly after Burke had stimulated the long-range missile program in 1955, the navy had discovered that a reliable solid-propellant fuel could be developed for a missile of 1,500-mile range. Subsequently, the Atomic Energy Commission learned that the weight of a nuclear warhead could be reduced considerably. The result of combining these disoveries was the Polaris missile, capable of being launched from a nuclear-propelled submarine. These submarines were very expensive, compared to a comparable number of weapons delivered by the B-52, but were relatively invulnerable, in comparison with any aircraft.

Not to be outdone in modernization, the air force struggled to retain its front position in the fiscal 1958 budget. The Symington Air Power Hearing Report, published in early 1957, was a major support in this struggle. What the hearings indicate is the air force's dissatisfaction with both the quantitative and qualitative aspects of force modernization, particularly the former: "Financial considerations have often been placed ahead of defense re-

quirements, to the serious damage of our airpower strength relative to that of Russia; and hence to our national security." [46]

Air Force Chief Nathan Twining attempted, without success,
to get the Joint Chiefs to go along with a requirement for six additional B-52 wings beyond the administration's program for fiscal year 1958 and accepted the negative decision with reluctance.
The Joint Chiefs of Staff were influenced, no doubt, by the fact
that the fiscal 1958 budget showed $4.2 billion for aircraft pro-
curement, as compared to only $2 billion for missile purchases.
The official air force position in 1957 on the future of bombers
in the age of missiles indicated no reduction in the bomber requirement: "Missiles, as they are perfected, will supplement and
complement the manned aircraft. However, to preserve the required capability and flexibility of operations, it is essential that
the Air Force maintain a significant force of manned aircraft
during the foreseeable future." [47]

The Eisenhower administration had an answer to the air force
critics. The answer was the notion of sufficiency, articulated by
Quarles in a magazine article. He used an analogy of two men,
bitter enemies, each confined to a room, and each with a grenade
in hand. Would giving one man a second grenade, he asked,
"alter the deterrent sufficiency of the other man's one grenade? I
think not." [48]

Meeting with the president in early November, just before the
presidential election of 1956, Wilson told Eisenhower that he had
a number of papers on unresolved disputes that needed to be
settled before the fiscal 1958 defense budget could be put in final
form.[49] After some discussion, it was decided that Wilson would
again meet with the president a day or two after the election. At
the subsequent meeting, Wilson presented a number of controversial problems pertaining to the budget, such as roles and missions, research and development, overseas deployments, force levels, and military assistance programs. After looking over a sum-
mary of the problems, the president said that "the questions were
largely technical, and would require his getting back into the
whole atmosphere of military planning." This he did not intend

to do. The discussion then proceeded to a rather general discussion of the defense budget.

By late November the estimates of the previous summer had been worked down to $43.4 billion; this was further pared by the Defense Department to an estimate of $39.6 billion by December 6. The following day there was a meeting with the president at Augusta, Georgia, on the defense budget. Wilson and Budget Director Percival F. Brundage were among those present, but neither the JCS nor its chairman was there.[50] In the analysis prepared by Brundage, the president noted that a major portion of the budget was in procurement, production, and construction. He felt it important to press for missile development, but to hold down procurement, since the main psychological significance came from the first few missiles developed. The president did agree to go ahead with a nuclear-powered carrier in order to test its operational characteristics, but felt a carrier every other year was sufficient. After considering the budget on a line basis, he asked Wilson to have it reduced to $38.5 billion.

On December 19 there was a meeting in the president's office on the military budget, at which the chairman and members of the Joint Chiefs of Staff were present. The president began with his familiar homily. In spending money for defense, he noted, one approached a point of "lessening returns or even of net loss." In the end this could lead to endangering the economy and, therefore, "weaken the country's overall position." He cited problems of inflation and the potential for another round of wage increases. While he realized that some members of the Joint Chiefs might be doubtful about the defense budget, in the end the budget became a matter of presidential decision. He averred that he was "by no means putting a dollar sign on defense," since there were, after all, other programs that were important to the country's strength. He felt he was the only person in a position to bring all this together, and in any case it would be impossible to pay for all the programs that were suggested. He felt that the figure of $38 billion would give adequate defense. This was about $4 billion above what had been anticipated about four years before, but it could not keep going up. He noted that Humphrey was deeply concerned about the U.S. economy, and possibly the government was being "reckless" about it.[51]

On December 21 the NSC met to ratify the fiscal year 1958 defense budget. After the presentation by Wilson and the services, the council agreed that the program was consistent with U.S. security policy objectives. The president pointed out that "for the remainder of his term in office he did not plan on going above $39 billion in any fiscal year." He qualified this by noting that this could be changed in the event of some "unforeseen emergency."[52]

By 1957 Wilson was quite familiar with the problems of handling the military bureaucracy, but still not certain of the answers. In early January of that year he met with Radford and some White House assistants on the problem of the chiefs' degree of commitment to the fiscal 1958 defense budget.[53] Wilson and Radford both felt that the chiefs did not believe they had agreed to the budget. They had stated a number of exceptions, and the air force had accepted the budget only as an "imposed ceiling." One of the White House assistants said the president had the opposite opinion, based upon his meeting with the chiefs. Radford acknowledged that the group did not speak up in their meeting with the president. Some of the Defense Department personnel were aware that one of the services was organizing to break down the budget by a series of "end runs" to Congress. Wilson was pessimistic about getting a solid service commitment to the budget during the congressional hearings. He pointed out that some military personnel felt that the president had not heard all the facts before making his decision. A White House aide felt that this was not the president's problem, but rather a problem for the Defense Department. This terminated the discussion.

As it turned out, a few days later an event galvanized congressional efforts to join the president in holding down the size of the defense budget. This was a news conference held by Treasury Secretary George Humphrey on January 15, 1957, in support of the new budget. In answering a question in the final minutes of the conference, he predicted a "depression that will curl your hair" if federal expenditures were not reduced. Humphrey was talking about long-range trends, but it was easy to interpret his predictions of a hair-curling depression in the context of the on-going budget action. The Democrats, who in the previous year had tried to force extra defense funds on the president, became, as Eisenhower later said, "inexplicably economy-minded."[54]

By March the House had passed a resolution asking the president to indicate where cuts in the budget could best be made. The president identified postponements rather than actual cuts. Subsequently, the House proposed a cut in the defense budget by some $2.5 billion, but in conference with the Senate this was reduced to $2.3 billion. The bulk of the cut came first from the army's budget, and then from the navy's; even the air force was cut some $500 million. While every category of defense appropriation was reduced to some extent, about half the total cut represented postponements until later fiscal years. Obviously, cutting the budget had become an exercise in its own right and was not based upon any systematic analysis of strategic requirements. In fact, there was no serious examination of the Eisenhower strategic policy by Congress at all; the cut was effected mostly on items that were, superficially, most amenable to postponement or reduction.

Eisenhower, realizing this economy wave would be short-lived, reminded Humphrey, Wilson, and Brundage that his NSC decision on future military budget ceilings announced at the December 21 NSC meeting had been designed to help Wilson keep the services in line.[55] The intent, he explained, was to avoid future high estimates such as the one received in the fiscal year 1958 budget preparation. Since the services would know the president's upper limit from the outset, Wilson would have a powerful lever against inflated budget requests.

President Eisenhower's activities and commentary in connection with the development of the fiscal years 1957 and 1958 defense budgets are further evidence of his views on the U.S. economy. The economy was central in his thinking on security matters. Logical argumentation, such as that in the great defense debates of the 1950s, was not enough to sway him from his defense budget ceiling.

This is not to say that Eisenhower did not have a strategic concept. He did, but it was different from that of his adversaries. Central to his thinking was the idea of strategic deterrent. When it came to local war, however, he differed with the theoretical writers and the army. It is clear that Eisenhower was prepared to use ground forces, but only to a certain level not specifically defined. After that he wanted to use tactical nuclear weapons. Eisenhower conceived of both tactical and strategic nuclear weapons in their operational mode as well as in their deterrent mode. Hence, all the talk about large-scale conventional warfare against the USSR was "fatuous." Even large-scale conventional warfare against a proxy would not be tolerated.

Certain techniques employed by Eisenhower to retain control of his strategy and of the defense budget emerge. He clearly recognized that his chief adversaries were the service chiefs and that they must not be permitted to break the appearance of consensus within the administration. To control the chiefs, he was careful during their selection process to give them a "loyalty" interview. Would they recognize that their duties came first? Would they leave the parochial service views to lesser officials, who could be controlled? Did they agree with the administration's strategic doctrine, and would they support it publicly?

Once on board, the Oval Office provided a good forum to keep the chiefs in line. They must take a broader view of the central importance of the economy to security. Those who could not take this broader view and play on the team should not hold their positions. In short, Dwight David Eisenhower considered not only the chairman of the JCS to be a political appointee, as he surely was, but also the military chiefs of service. The professional—or parochial—view of the chiefs must never interfere with their support of the administration in strategy or defense budget ceilings.

Finally, the importance to Eisenhower's decision-making process of the sessions in the president's office with ad hoc groups is clear. The formal NSC sessions were important for coordination and for developing teamwork, but the decisions were not generally talked out there. They had already been made in the president's office.

## CHAPTER THREE

# *After Sputnik*

EVENTS DURING the years 1957–1959 were challenging for President Eisenhower and for his strategic concepts, as well as the defense budgets that were developed to implement those concepts. Always a popular president, he was, nevertheless, subject to increasing criticisms and pressures related to his handling of domestic and international problems as his second term progressed.[1] Domestic pressures centered around the 1957–1958 recession and the congressional elections of 1958. In the international context, a more assertive Soviet thrust, symbolized both by the Soviet challenge over Berlin and by the launching of Sputnik, was evident. Notwithstanding increasing pressures from the military bureaucracy, Congress, and certain writers to increase the allocation of resources to defense, Eisenhower was determined to retain both his strategic concepts and his tight control on the defense budget.

There had been a recession in 1953–1954 that the administration had weathered fairly well, but the recession of 1957–1958 was a sterner test. Between October 1957 and February 1958, unemployment more than doubled, reaching 7.7 percent of the labor force. From the administration's point of view, the chief threat was inflation. Accordingly attempts were made to confine remedies to fiscal, monetary, and credit actions that would not increase inflationary forces. In particular, Eisenhower's advisers wanted to avoid a massive public works program and a tax cut at that time. Some actions were taken, however, that constituted a mild, but temporary, departure from the fiscal orthodoxy that in general characterized the Eisenhower administration. Democrats displayed more initiative than they had in the earlier recession and generally opposed the administration's approach, with the main conflict taking place as part of the legislative process. Eventually the economy recovered, but the Republican party paid the price in the 1958 congressional elections.[2]

These elections were a disaster for the Republican party. This can be attributed partly to organizational weaknesses, but there were also specific issues that did not help the Republican image with certain groups of voters. On the domestic scene, in addition to the recession, these issues were the use of troops to integrate a high school in Little Rock in September 1957, Sherman Adams's departure under a cloud just before the election, Secretary of Agriculture Ezra Benson's farm program, and the activities of labor organizations against the administration. Voter perception of the international scene did not help—especially Sputnik and the newly announced "missile gap." In a Gallup poll in October 1956, a question was asked about the party best able to keep the United States out of war. Response was 42 percent for the Republicans and 17 percent for the Democrats. In August 1958 the same question scored 26 percent for the Republicans and 24 percent for the Democrats. Korea was fading from view, and the new technology of missiles was very much in view.

The balance of party representation in Congress can be misleading. Much of the real opposition to the administration on foreign policy came from the Republican party. In reality, Eisenhower had no party of his own in terms of support for his foreign policy, but had to rely heavily on Democrats throughout all four Congresses. This is illustrated by Hans Morgenthau, writing in 1958: "[This situation] was symbolized in the paradoxical po-

sition of Senator Knowland who, as majority and [later, as] minority leader in the Senate, had the official function to rally his
party to the support of the President's foreign policies and who
by conviction was the most outspoken critic of them." [3]

When it came to defense budgets, however, voting more closely
followed party lines. In the eight years of the administration, on
twelve roll-call votes, a majority of the Democrats twice supported the administration and ten times opposed it. In all twelve
cases a majority of congressional Republicans supported the
administration. [4]

When Sputnik I was orbited by the Soviets in October 1957,
they had a great opportunity to exploit this technological feat at
the psychological expense of the United States. The resulting
"missile gap" debate is pertinent here, because it eventually over-
whelmed other defense issues in public debate and simultaneously diverted potential support and interest from the limited
war concept, which, by 1957, had gained substantial attention as
an issue.

Sputnik dramatized the technological gains of the Soviet
Union. Khrushchev became the chief Soviet spokesman in exploiting this psychological advantage. Initially, this took the form
of a claim that the U.S. strategic advantage had been, or was
being, nullified. Sputnik provided an aura of credibility for
claims of a big Soviet ICBM program. The Russians soon claimed
ICBM production and shortly thereafter claimed an operational
capability in ICBMs. [5]

The Soviet space achievements and their claims of growing
ICBM capability were increasingly debated in the U.S. press and
Congress. The debate became particularly intense in connection
with the 1958 congressional elections. It continued in 1959 and
eventually became a major issue in the 1960 presidential campaign. Eisenhower took the position that although the Soviet
Union led in certain areas of research and production, the overall U.S. capability was adequate for deterrence. Insofar as there
was a gap, Eisenhower traced it to the Truman period and stated
it was speedily being closed. [6]

In all the charges and countercharges surrounding the "missile gap," one point was not well known until the spring of 1960. Throughout the controversy Eisenhower had available to him photography taken from a U-2 plane. While this told more of current capabilities than it did of future Soviet intentions, the fact is that Eisenhower had valuable sources on which to base his estimates of Soviet strategic delivery means. Nevertheless, the "missile gap" controversy did have an impact on both strategic policy and budgetary allocations.

During this period Soviet leadership attempted to exploit the decreasing credibility of the U.S. deterrent for the defense of Western Europe. Khrushchev boasted of the USSR's ability to destroy the European NATO countries. His major attempt at exploiting his psychological advantage was the Berlin crisis, which he initiated in November of 1958. Eisenhower saw no need to modify his basic deterrent policy, anymore than he had a few months earlier in the squabble over the Chinese offshore islands of Quemoy and Matsu.[7]

In only one instance, the 102-day operation in Lebanon in July 1958, did Eisenhower commit substantial U.S. forces in an international conflict—about fifteen thousand marine and army troops equipped with conventional weapons. By late October, all U.S. troops had withdrawn without having been in direct military action. In his memoirs Eisenhower had some interesting comments on the military aspect of this affair:

On the military side the Lebanon operation demonstrated the ability of the United States to react swiftly with conventional armed forces to meet small-scale, or "brush fire" situations. . . .

The Lebanon operation was not to be compared to the serious fighting of the Korean War. But such operations had convinced me that if "small wars" were to break out in several places simultaneously, then we would not fight on the enemy's terms and be limited to his choice of weapons.[8]

However much it might be modified by rhetoric, the massive retaliation concept remained the essence of U.S. strategy in the NATO area during the period 1957–1959. Nevertheless, the higher military command of NATO took some initiative to be less dependent on immediate nuclear retaliation. General Lauris Norstad, of the air force, who became supreme commander in late 1956, was successful in getting the council to adopt MC 70 in 1957. This was a five-year plan designed to create a force of thirty divisions on the central front in Western Europe. The main justification for this force was to promise a pause of sufficient duration to compel the USSR to make a deliberate choice between halting a conventional probe and going to all-out nuclear war. The projected additional forces were thus viewed as providing flexibility, but not the ability to fight a conventional war in Western Europe. The thirty-division force requirement was only about half-met by the end of 1959.[9]

One issue that caused increased problems with the NATO allies in the wake of Sputnik was nuclear-sharing. Sputnik dramatized the potential vulnerability of the United States to the missiles of the USSR. Naturally, the allies were uncomfortable adjusting to the new reality that their defense was ultimately dependent upon a country which was vulnerable itself to nuclear attack. One allied reaction was a desire to have a larger share in the control of the nuclear capability on which their defense was based. A *New York Times* article of November 14, 1957, was headlined "NATO Allies Bid U.S. and Britain Share Atom Arms." Further down in the article was a quotation from a French general who summed up this position rather well: "However solid may be the ties that unite the signatory states of the North Atlantic Treaty, the risk created by the appearance of the absolute weapon . . . is now too grave to permit . . . a single one of the allies the monopoly of a retaliation which in the hour of danger, could be neutralized by the enemy or by the opposition of its own press or public opinion."

The United States' response to both Sputnik and allied qualms came at the NATO council meeting the following month. The council accepted a United States offer to deploy intermediate range missiles in Europe subject to the agreement of the countries concerned. This was a temporary measure to deter the Soviets until American intercontinental missiles were operational. Only Britain and Turkey eventually accepted the offer.

In an attempt to expand nuclear-sharing, and perhaps alleviate allied concerns, the council also accepted the United States' offer to participate in a NATO atomic stockpile. This was in effect the offer Dulles had made the previous December in which the United States would retain custody of the warheads themselves. The offer as restated added that in event of hostilities the warheads would be released to the allies.

Eisenhower always wanted to go further with interallied cooperation on planning and control of atomic weapons. However, congressional inhibitions frustrated him on this. As he himself later put it: "If the President had in the field of nuclear affairs the same authority he had in other areas the problem could be readily resolved. The difficulty arises in that the Joint Committee on Atomic Energy . . . wants to keep nuclear science as a special preserve." Even the modest nuclear-sharing granted NATO in December 1957, felt Eisenhower, required him to have a meeting with congressional leaders to be certain he had their support.[10]

There was considerable continuity in individuals who shaped the first and second Eisenhower administrations. John Foster Dulles remained as secretary of state until cancer immobilized him in the early months of 1959. Throughout his term as secretary, the problem of Soviet intentions remained central in his thinking. Yet there were changes in his outlook over time: a less critical attitude toward neutrals and perhaps some disenchantment with massive retaliation as a concept, at least in the manner he originally articulated it. His rapport with the president, already great by 1955, never waned. Nor did his penchant for being connected with unfortunate phrases. An article in *Life* magazine, after an interview with him, added "going to the brink" and "brinkmanship" to the cold war vocabulary. Perhaps this was his way of simplifying complex issues so as to build public support for administration policies. On the other hand, perhaps it was evidence of a characteristic that his successor

Christian Herter saw in him, when comparing himself and Dulles: "I think perhaps the major difference between ourselves was my own feeling that the President was the Constitutional officer responsible for foreign affairs. Whether he made the policy or didn't make the policy, he ought to be out in front in connection with it; and I didn't want it to be known as a Herter policy, I'd much rather have it an Eisenhower policy. I think Foster rather liked it being a Dulles policy." [11]

There was a large military component in Dulles's policies, but how much he understood the military aspects is debatable. Two of the service chiefs, Taylor and Burke, thought Dulles's knowledge of military matters was not as great as it should be. Maxwell Taylor felt Dulles never really looked carefully at the military instrument being welded at the Pentagon. In effect, he did not ask the big questions on military strategy. Arleigh Burke came away from a meeting with Dulles with the same opinion. [12]

Treasury Secretary Humphrey remained irrepressible and fiscally conservative to the day of his departure from the administration in July 1957. An observer remembers one of his parting shots in the NSC this way: "I realize we have to spend $38 billion on defense right now, but if we keep it up year after year, we're going to have real trouble." [13]

Apparently Humphrey's influence with the president continued long after he left office. There was no question in Humphrey's mind where the main problem with defense budgets was, as he viewed it from the vantage point of 1964: "and very frankly, some of the Army generals caused most of the trouble. They were . . . from my point of view just Army-minded morning, noon, and night. If you gave a nickel to anybody the Army had to have a lot more." [14]

Robert B. Anderson, Humphrey's successor at the Treasury, had served previously as both secretary of the navy and deputy defense secretary. Still a relatively young man, he was a lawyer and estate manager in Texas before entering government. Apparently somewhat more flexible than Humphrey, he was equally conservative in his economic philosophy. He was not as ebullient as Humphrey, but he was both tenacious in argument and adroit in negotiations. Although not part of the president's bridge-playing or quail-shooting coterie, there is no question of the high esteem in which Eisenhower held him. In his memoirs Eisenhower mentions him as a potential vice presidential candidate and secretary of state. There seems to be no question that he was one of the economically conservative forces of the second administration.[15]

Charles Wilson's tour as secretary of defense lasted almost five years. As time went on his effectiveness diminished. He had no real rapport with the president. His penchant for the colorful but politically disastrous phrase continued as a liability.[16] Wilson was strong on management ability and weak on strategic understanding. Another characteristic of Wilson was a tendency to get the president more involved in Pentagon business than he wanted to be. This is easy to understand, considering Wilson's role as business manager of the defense establishment. Out of the mainstream of the strategic dialogue, and yet making budgetary decisions that could have considerable impact on strategic capabilities, Wilson's only alternatives were to turn to the president or be wholly dependent on the chairman of the JCS.

Wilson's successor, Neil Hosler McElroy, arrived in the office at a difficult time, being sworn in less than a week after Sputnik and just in time for the final efforts on the fiscal year 1959 defense budget. McElroy apparently was surprised at being selected for the job and accepted it on the basis that he would serve no more than two years. His previous career, most recently as president of Procter and Gamble, had been concerned with the promotion and sale of soap. In this regard he had less relevant background to defense activities than had Wilson as president of General Motors. Like Wilson, he can also be regarded as a functionalist in his approach to the secretary's role. He did have one distinct advantage over Wilson, his public personality. As he himself put it: "I think maybe I was a little more accustomed to dealing with the public than Charley was." [17]

Like Wilson, McElroy relied on his subordinates to see that

the president's policies were carried out. He also felt that he could instill in the service chiefs a sense of being good businessmen.[18] In neither case was his judgment correct. There was a jingle that went the rounds in the Pentagon in those days: "Nothing is ever complete, neither victory nor defeat." When a service received an adverse decision it did not, like a subordinate agency in Procter and Gamble, simply carry it out. It used its many faceted apparatus to attempt to get the decision changed. As for being good businessmen, that was all right if it did not interfere with a service chief's professional views. After all, his role was the essence of military professionalism; he was not in the profit-and-loss business.

McElroy's arrival with Sputnik forced him into a number of significant hardware decisions at the outset. He projected a good image in making these decisions. As time went on, though, he gave the appearance of vacillation, and his image in his second year was less impressive. In any case, two years is too short a period for a defense secretary, especially one without a defense background, to become truly effective. His role was essentially the same as Wilson's; only the outward personalities were different.

The summer of 1957 brought the retirement of Admiral Arthur Radford. For four years he had been an able advocate of the administration's position on defense matters. Highly effective and respected by the president, Dulles, Humphrey, and Wilson, his was the tough job of working routinely with the service chiefs. Only one of these did Radford consider cooperative, and that was Nathan Twining, who succeeded him as chairman.

Twining's approach as chairman was apparently somewhat less partisan than Radford's had been. Admiral Arleigh Burke had absolute confidence that Twining, in representing the chiefs, would tell the entire story. As air force chief, however, Twining had been an advocate of the massive retaliation concept and was unlikely either to change that view or to favor any attempts at a new strategic appraisal. Although his basic professional interests were in strategic bombardment, he seemed to appreciate more than Radford the efforts of the other services. He remained, however, highly loyal to Eisenhower and his strategic policies. Many years after his retirement he wrote a rather curious book in which he gave the Eisenhower defense efforts high marks, except for "a tendency to allow a gradual erosion of U.S. military posture through partial accommodation to . . . pressure groups who were working for unilateral disarmament, the abolition of nuclear weapons, and the denial of the medium of space for military operations." [19]

General Thomas Dresser White was Twining's successor as chief of staff of the air force. He had been Twining's vice chief for the preceding four years, so there was no break in the continuity of air force leadership. There were senior air force generals, in particular, General Otto Weyland, head of the Tactical Air Command, who believed in the possibility of local nonatomic war, but they were not in power in the air force. Normally those in power would state that if a local requirement developed, SAC could handle it without lessening its general war capabilities. The White House and air force continued in harmony on overall priorities. From about 1956 on, however, they began to draw apart on how much strategic capability was enough. The administration, with an eye on the budget, decided on sufficiency. The air force wanted to maintain a counterforce strategy, which, in the light of increasing Soviet strategic capabilities, would have been very expensive indeed.

Preparation of the 1957 budget had been characterized by the air force offensive to accelerate force modernization. The following year had been the year of the economy mood; and, although it did not start that way, preparation of the fiscal year 1959 budget became the year of Sputnik. In July and August 1957, the economy mood of the previous year was still predominant. In July the president met with Wilson and his new deputy, Donald Quarles, to go over the guidelines for the 1959 budget. One of the key issues was manpower, and Wilson hoped to get total military strength down from 2.8 to 2.5 million.[20] The president generally agreed with the figure, although he was uncertain how the cuts should be allocated among the services. Wilson, by now highly sensitive to Congress and the military bureaucracy, thought it might be good if the president were to meet soon with leaders in both agencies to discuss the new program. As far as Congress was concerned, Eisenhower felt that for the moment letters would do. In the case of the Joint Chiefs of Staff, the president thought it much too early for him to discuss specific manpower decisions. "The chiefs would know that I was being purely arbitrary" to make a decision of this type at such an early date. Further, it was too early to release projected manpower figures. He turned out to be correct because in less than three months the Soviets had orbited Sputnik.

The psychological and strategic impact of Sputnik has been described extensively in literature on that period. Obviously, Sputnik affected the defense budget. The economy mood of the previous year was now something of an embarrassment, particularly to Congress. The president, however, was not one to overreact, especially when it came to defense spending. On October 9, less than a week after Sputnik, Neil McElroy was sworn in as Wilson's replacement, as previously planned. After the ceremony the president invited the Pentagon leaders to his office to talk about what attitude to maintain in view of the Sputnik situation.[21] He reminded everyone that separating U.S. military missile effort from the U.S. scientific effort, which was designed to lead to an orbiting, had been intentional. When the military began to say, as some recently had, that certain of their missiles could have placed a satellite in orbit earlier, they tended to give the impression of a race, which he felt was wrong. He wanted the Pentagon leaders to avoid comments on this matter whenever possible.

It would probably have been impossible, however, for the services not to have viewed the developing public and congressional concern as a favorable climate for increased emphasis on force modernization and larger defense budgets. In a subsequent private meeting with the president, the new defense secretary brought up the budget limit of $38 billion and said he would like not to regard it as a ceiling. The president agreed and added that he "had not wished to establish a figure at all but had done so on the repeated request of Secretary Wilson."

On October 30 McElroy met with the president to discuss the defense budget. The defense secretary felt that after his personnel briefed the president on the budget, there should be an opportunity for the service secretaries and chiefs to meet with Eisenhower so that they could mention deficiencies as they saw them.[22] The president again stated his views on the responsibility of the top defense officials to consider the broader aspects of the budget. "If the budget is too high, inflation occurs, which in effect cuts down the value of the dollar, so that nothing is gained, and the process is self-defeating." As far as military manpower was concerned, it was Eisenhower's aim to come down from 2.8 to 2.5 million and still have a stronger force. Such innovations as the army's Pentomic Division would assist in accomplishing this objective. His goal was to find a stable budget ceiling at which the defense budget could be kept, barring inflation or adverse developments. The president noted that "last year although the chiefs accepted a certain figure, they so organized their programs as to initiate a large amount of work which would cost much more to carry on this year."

One facet that McElroy wanted to emphasize to the president was new service perceptions of their modernization requirements and the possibility of getting them funded in the light of Sputnik—for example, the decision by Eisenhower in October 1953 to accept continental air defense as a major strategic program. By 1957 two main schools of thought had developed with respect to air defense. One argued that active defense was impossible especially after Sputnik demonstrated that the Soviet strategic threat in the future would be missiles and not aircraft. Further, this view, which was espoused by the air force, argued that resources should be used to strengthen and enlarge SAC so that its ability to retaliate instantly was increasingly improved. This they concluded would be the greatest deterrent and greatest defense against any Soviet strategic initiative.

The other school of thought, espoused by the army, concluded that an active defense was possible and they thought they had the answer in their proposed third generation surface-to-air missile—Nike-Zeus. The *New York Times* of October 29, 1957, reporting on speeches by Maxwell Taylor and other high-ranking army generals summarized the army's position as follows: "Major emphasis should now be placed on developing a defense against intercontinental missiles, rather than on retaliatory air power to prevent an enemy attack."[23]

The NSC and Defense Department had tended, as a matter of expediency, to favor passive defense measures against the ICBM, combined with the U.S. strategic deterrent, and national policy papers on continental defense implied that an active defense was not possible. This was an issue that was to continue unanswered for many years. In the immediate post-Sputnik period, the army's goal was to secure funding to allow it to move Nike-Zeus within a year or two from development to production. In this they never succeeded with President Eisenhower. The army's concept was eventually accepted to the point of being given a high priority in national policy papers, but this was never translated into sufficient funding to initiate production planning, until the antiballistic missile a decade earlier.

The month before Sputnik, while the economy mood still prevailed, the chief of naval operations, Arleigh Burke, talked at the Naval War College on the economy as a pillar of U.S. strength. "Military appetites have to conform to the economic facts of life," was the theme he stressed. By December, when he was speaking to naval flag officers in Washington, his theme had changed. Early in his talk, Burke stated that the launching of the Russian satellite had made "a lot of people" receptive to new ideas of all kinds, including, he implied, larger defense budgets and new strategic concepts.[24]

Two problems Burke especially stressed in this talk were the role of the carrier and the role of limited-war forces. After outlining the arguments used against carriers, he went on to highlight points that the navy leaders could use in countering those arguments. Even though a new carrier was not in the 1959 budget, Burke had managed to keep in $35 million for carrier items with long-lead times, with the thought of requesting additional amounts in the next budget. He concluded: "But the fight is not over. The next big battle will be in Congress—and with a satellite-conscious Congress—the carrier will have to be justified with everything we've got."[25]

By this time the navy was fully backing the limited-war option. Burke warned his listeners that the dramatic accomplishments of the Soviets in satellites were having a psychological impact on a lot of influential people. He told the assembled flag officers that they had "the grave responsibility of insuring that attention is not so fully diverted . . . that we sacrifice our ability to deal with the more likely localized problem."[26] The point was that the navy had the built-in flexibility to cope with both forms of warfare, he stated. Therefore, force modernization provided equipment inherently useful for all levels of war.

In the immediate post-Sputnik period SAC had two pressing modernization issues. First was modernizing the bomber force itself. This program was based on two separate developments designed to reduce the effectiveness of Soviet antiaircraft defenses: the discovery that it was feasible to conduct low-level attacks with the B-52, which provided some protection from Soviet defenses; and rapid progress being made in research on a turbojet missile that could be delivered on targets from B-52s, without the aircraft themselves entering the defended areas.[27]

The second major modernization issue was the early attainment of an effective ICBM capability. The air force missile program at that time envisioned deployment of liquid-fueled Thor and Jupiter IRBMs (Intermediate Range Ballistic Missiles) to Europe between 1958 and 1960. The liquid-fueled Atlas and Titan ICBM would be developed and deployed in the United States over a five-year period. McElroy was inclined to be cautious about this latter program. His missile advisers apparently were optimistic about development of solid-propellant ICBMs and did not want to build up inventories of early model missiles. McElroy felt there would be no gap in U.S. defenses in the interim.

Superimposed on the normal presidential discussions on the

defense budget at this time of the year there came, in 1957, the Gaither Committee report, which gained considerable attention.[28] The committee, made up of private citizens, was formed to study problems in the area of continental defense in general and shelter programs in particular. After a series of technical studies were completed during the summer of 1957, the group met in Washington during the fall. Like many similar panels, they decided to broaden their interests to include the entire range of U.S. defense programs. By the end of October the group was ready to brief the president on its findings.

Robert Cutler, presidential assistant, gave the president a preliminary report on October 29 indicating that the group was proposing expensive programs and should brief him. The president said he was beginning to wonder whether such groups should be established. The danger he saw was that the group would put out a lot of alarmist talk. On November 4 the group came to the president's office for the briefing. The report was far-ranging, and here we can only concentrate on certain aspects. The group felt that the strategic air force was highly vulnerable to the Soviet's ICBM, and the U.S. population critically vulnerable. They felt that the United States should increase its strategic offensive power through the introduction of a diversified group of missiles. The committee did not stop with strategic forces; it also recommended improvements in preparation for conventional local war. The committee assigned a very low priority to constructing shelters. On this point Eisenhower agreed, seeing the shelter program as "a local activity."[29]

After listening to its recommendations, the president said, "All military strength is relative to what a possible adversary has." He went on to say he "thought our strategic forces are stronger than the group may have indicated." He was inclined to think that whatever efforts were put into modernizing defenses should be directed toward protection of strategic forces. One matter he felt the group had not addressed was the question of long-range public support for the kind of accelerated defense effort they were proposing. He felt that getting the public to carry indefinite defense burdens would be a most difficult problem. He also believed that simply to call for a spurt of activity at this point would be the wrong approach. "The crux is, therefore, how to keep up interest and support without hysteria." The problem, he said, was going to be with the country until the Soviets changed, and this might be forty years.

The president noted that we had the ability to inflict 50 percent casualties on the enemy. "In those circumstances," he told the group, "there is in reality no defense except to retaliate." He concluded, "Maximum massive retaliation remains the crux of our defense." Continental air defense and conventional forces might be major strategic programs, but resources were not going to be increased greatly for these programs as long as the United States had the ability to inflict massive retaliation on the Soviet Union. That was the solution to the defense problem as Eisenhower saw it.

On November 7 the president presided at an NSC meeting at which the report was presented and discussed. It was an interesting report, Eisenhower said, with a number of good ideas, but could not be accepted as a guide for action.[30] The panel, he felt, had failed to take into account a number of important matters, including the question of priorities.

Later, portions of the report were leaked to the press and a clamor arose, especially in Congress, for the release of the entire report. No doubt the leaks were inspired by some members of the administration who were interested in higher defense spending. No doubt, also, it was one of the pressures that eventually did lead to increasing the defense budget. On the issue of releasing the report, however, the president was adamant. The answer was no. The president considered the report a confidential advisory opinion to him. He "could see no national advantage in broadcasting the opinions and suppositions in the report with the attendant risks to security."[31]

To help counter public anxiety over the Soviet launchings and the attendant public commentary, the president decided to give three "confidence" speeches to the American public. The third was never given because of an intervening illness, the second stressed the promotion of basic scientific research, and the first, given on November 7, was entitled, "Science and National Security." The major points made by the president were that the overall military strength of the free world was greater than that of the Communist countries and that the United States must be selective in expending its resources.[32]

One means employed by the president to generate harmony and compromise was a kind of high-level therapy session known as the stag dinner. President Eisenhower held such an affair in early November 1957, which was attended by the secretaries and chiefs of the military departments. After dinner he began a seminar by saying that the people he had met with that day all had stressed their concern over rivalry in the military establishment.[33] One of the basic questions, he felt, was "are we getting the best personal judgment of our officers, rather than a parroting of service party lines." Air Force Chief White said he felt that charges of rivalry were least realistic in the area of missiles.

Although there had been competition, he felt that it had produced good results. Regardless of who develops a missile, it is clear which service will operate it. General Taylor affirmed that although the army was developing the 1,500-mile Jupiter, it would be turned over to the air force to operate. Taylor added that the army does have a requirement for a shorter-range missile. Chairman Twining indicated that the army was to have no missile more than 200 miles in range. The president said he "did not accept the idea of such a fixed range limitation." He felt the army missile agency should take advantage of new developments that give possibilities of added range. Later it could be determined how the resulting weapon could best be used.

The discussion then turned to matters of organization. The president stated that while he did not regard organization as an answer in itself, it could sometimes be used to lead individuals to take a broader outlook. In this regard he thought the members of the JCS should turn over the executive direction of their service to their vice chiefs and concentrate on their joint responsibilities. He recalled previous discussions with the JCS, when he had urged them "to take the stance of soldier-statesmen." He then asked for their further comments.

Admiral Burke said "he would venture to disagree on some aspects of the president's proposal." The individual chiefs, he said, have different backgrounds and experiences. He thought that the disagreements did not arise because of service affiliations, but because of these different backgrounds. Further, many of the major problems "were not susceptible of final solution, but must be worked at day by day." General Taylor said he thought the real problem was budgetary. Further, to give executive direction of the services to the vice chiefs would require a major overhaul of the command structure.

Deputy Defense Secretary Quarles agreed that the essence of the problem was budgetary. Each service receives an appropriation from Congress, and to increase this budget it is natural for the service to appeal to the people and to the Congress. The key, said Quarles, was sufficient reorganization to have all appropriations made to the Defense Department itself. That agency could then apportion out the appropriations to the services in what it considered to be the optimal proportions.

The president said he felt the country was disturbed over the security situation. He thought that many people had come to believe "that the services were more interested in the struggle with each other, than against an outside foe." Those picked to serve in the top joint positions must have a national spirit and outlook. It was "deeply disappointing," said Eisenhower, "to see any of these top individuals devoting himself to his own service interests." The president concluded the meeting by saying the secretaries and chiefs must stand firmly behind the administration's defense program, even though it might not fully meet any service's desires.

Meanwhile, the president continued to be involved in meetings on the fiscal year 1959 defense budget. Meeting in his office with McElroy on November 11, he said he thought that "the [aircraft] carrier has about run its course."[34] He realized that this was a controversial point and that there was some utility in carriers, but their vulnerability to nuclear weapons impressed him. Particularly was this so in small areas, such as the Mediterranean. McElroy pointed out their great value in local war situations or shows of force. The president agreed, but felt the existing carriers were adequate for such purposes. On the overall defense budget, he felt he could defend some increases providing the total remained below $40 billion. However, in handling the matter in the NSC he felt it should be done by beginning with a $38 billion budget and then determining what might be the deficiencies.

On the fifteenth, McElroy was back to see Eisenhower, and said that Gates (secretary of navy) and Burke would like to see the president before any decision was made on the question of carriers.[35] The president felt the answer was to defer any decision on another carrier for a year. McElroy felt the navy would accept that approach in order to gain possibly stronger support later. The president felt that the Defense Department might be "pushing the Navy a little too much at the expense of the Army." He saw some advantage to taking the carrier out of the fiscal 1959 program and giving the army an additional allowance for some of their perceived needs.

On November 22 the president met with McElroy in his office immediately following a cabinet meeting, in order to discuss some points concerning the military budget. He wanted to approach all budget decisions not on the basis of public pressure but rather on the basis of the real need for the item in question.[36] He stressed that defense requirements were relative to the Soviet Union's posture. Since "Soviet ICBMs would not overmatch our bomber power in the next few years," the U.S. defense pace should be based on good sense and a calm reading of the objective situation of the Soviet Union.

The focus of defense budget sessions in December 1957, two months after Sputnik, was different from that in previous years. The problem for the administration was to convey a public image of understanding the new threat, and moving to meet it, without departing significantly from the budgetary constraints that had previously been in effect.

One issue was how to expedite the completion of two first-generation IRBMs, the air force's Thor and the army's Jupiter, in such a way as to project an image of initiative on the part of the administration. A meeting was held on the matter in the president's office in early December. Those attending included the vice president, Dulles, McElroy, and others from the White House and Defense Department staffs.[37] Dulles was curious whether the military considered the accelerated program to be adequate and whether they would back it. The question in his mind was whether the military thought there would be a period during 1959 when the United States would be exposed to the Soviets—whether SAC bombers would be adequate during that period. McElroy pointed out that such a Soviet threat was not a certainty, but at most a probability. Then Dulles wanted to know whether the bomber force would be adequate through 1960, even if the Soviets deployed missiles that could cover Western Europe. The main question he felt the Europeans had was whether the United States was keeping up technologically. It was not, he felt, that they wanted missiles themselves. Dulles added that perhaps the more significant problem was not with the Europeans, but with the American people, "who felt exposed to attack for the first time." There were no clear answers to the questions raised by Dulles, but the decision was made to go ahead with an accelerated Thor-Jupiter program.

On January 9, 1958, Eisenhower's State of the Union message conveyed the feeling that a large expansion in defense efforts was in the making: "Every part of our military establishment must and will be equipped to do its defensive job with the most modern weapons and methods." The budget message of January 13, however, emphasized expenditures for defense but seemed to indicate a more orderly approach, similar to that exhibited in the meetings previously discussed.[38] Eisenhower requested a supplemental appropriation to the 1958 budget of $1.3 billion in spending authority and a further increase of $2.5 billion in fiscal 1959 over 1958, to be applied principally to strategic programs. In other areas, especially tactical forces, there were to be decreases in modernization efforts. The emphasis was on missiles, bombers, and nuclear weapons. That spring there were two more supplemental requests for fiscal 1959, one in April for $1.45 billion and one in June for $0.6 billion. The air force was the principal beneficiary of these increases, but they still did not receive as much as air force leaders had wanted.

The increased emphasis on technology reflected in the 1959 defense budget was potentially threatening to other parts of the budget, such as the economic aid program. This was of some concern to Dulles, and at a meeting of bipartisan congressional leaders with the president, Dulles had an opportunity to get across his point. His strategic formulation is interesting, since it is primarily addressed to a potential budget problem in foreign aid. There were, he felt, three pressures from the Soviets, the first being their threats and readiness to risk general war.[39] For this the United States had a deterrent strategy, the capacity for massive retaliation. The second pressure was the Soviet capability for local war. Here the allies must provide the defense, with U.S. air and sea support. Finally, the USSR could employ the technique of subversion, for which the United States had programs of economic aid and information. In his opinion, Dulles told the congressmen, subversion posed "the greatest danger" from the Soviet Union.

Numerous individuals who have commented on Dulles's strategic concepts have emphasized how in his later years as secretary his thinking began to range beyond massive retaliation. There is also evidence of pressures within his own department to adopt more flexible strategic notions.[40] In fact, Gerard Smith tells of persuading Dulles that something along those lines had to be done, and of Dulles's subsequent meeting with defense representatives in the Pentagon.

The meeting took place in the office of the secretary of defense in early April 1958, with a large number of principals in attendance. McElroy indicated that the group had assembled at the president's request to consider a matter that Dulles had raised.[41] At this point Dulles explained that for some years he had been a supporter of the massive retaliation concept. Now he thought that "new conditions were emerging which while not invalidating the massive retaliation concept" might require its being supplemented. The new conditions were developments in Soviet strategic hardware, combined with some skepticism on the part of allies concerning U.S. determination actually to use strategic weapons in light of these Soviet weapons developments. The question in his mind was whether or not tactical atomic weapons provided a supplementary concept that gave greater credibility to U.S. strategic policy.

McElroy indicated that a central question was whether tactical atomic weapons could be used without escalating into the use of larger nuclear weapons. Twining indicated that small weapons were being developed, but they were not adequate to stop a large-scale attack. Burke, demonstrating a new emphasis for the navy, indicated there was a need to develop the capacity for smaller operations. Taylor pointed out that tactical nuclear weapons offer major possibilities, but at the moment the variety in the inventory was not great.

At this point the deputy secretary of defense, Donald Quarles, interjected that he thought the massive retaliation concept was inescapable. He felt that defense technology had not gained in relation to offense technology through the development of nuclear weapons. Dulles felt there was a need for doctrines on tactical weapons, since all-out war was so awesome there was the possibility that a decision to undertake it might not be taken. Gates posed the question: if the deterrent fails to deter, then what should the retaliatory force be designed to accomplish? Twining said this required some flexibility. The correct targets are industrial and communications centers, but if restricted to military targets, then larger numbers of weapons would be needed. Dulles concluded with the hope that something concrete could be developed which could be presented to the allies.

This was, all in all, an interesting session. One can see how Taylor might think Dulles would side with him in a strategy session in the NSC several months later on the annual revision of the BNSP. In this session, Taylor took the lead in advocating greater emphasis for limited war. As Taylor recounts it in his book, however, Dulles remained silent after Taylor's presentation to the president of the need for a more flexible strategy. In this instance, Taylor felt he was also acting as spokesman for the navy and marine corps. Gerard Smith confirms that the secretary of state failed to support Taylor on this occasion.[42] This was, however, a different forum from that in McElroy's office in one important respect. Dwight Eisenhower, architect and still proponent of a nuclear-heavy strategy, was present. Dulles does not emerge as the major figure in strategic policy development that he is sometimes held out to be, particularly after the first years of the administration.

Meanwhile, in Congress, questioning of the administration was wide-ranging and generally critical. There was no disagreement on the need to strengthen the strategic forces; the issue was, by how much. Appropriations were increased over the administration's request in the case of Polaris and two air force missile programs. There was less agreement on improving limited-war capabilities, although some additional money over that requested by the president was voted for army modernization, airlift capacity, and army and marine corps personnel strength. In the end Congress voted the administration $0.8 billion more than the president had requested.

In late June 1958 there was a meeting in the president's office to consider a proposed administration position on increased appropriations voted at that point only by the House.[43] McElroy said it was his belief that appropriations were merely authorizations, and not mandates to spend. The defense comptroller, Wilfred McNeil, suggested not taking any public position for or against the funds, but simply handling the matter administratively. The president felt everyone in the administration should understand that "the [additional] funds would be spent only when the need for such expenditure had been determined by proper authority."

Thus the 1959 budget was developed in circumstances quite different from the economy mood of the previous year because of what some perceived as an extraordinary change in the international context. The president still believed, however, that holding down the defense budget was more important than the changing context or any rational argumentation to change strategic policy in reaction to that context.

While the post-Sputnik budget and strategy meetings were being held, the president was busy with another approach designed to give him better control over the defense policy and budgetary processes. To Eisenhower the organization of the Defense Department seemed to leave something to be desired. The public and Congress also were uneasy about the frequent, sometimes daily, accounts of duplication among the military services. With the impetus of Sputnik, all these apprehensions came together in a general agreement that the Defense Department needed further reorganization. Typical of these feelings was a remark made by John McCloy of the Gaither panel when that group met with the president in early November 1957.[44] McCloy felt that there was clearly a need for organizational improvement in the Defense Department. Interservice rivalry had now reached the point, he said, that it "was spreading to industries and universities" affiliated with particular services. Eisenhower agreed and articulated some of the organizational proposals he had in mind, such as taking the services out of operational command and integrating the Joint Staff.

In the same month the Rockefeller Committee on Governmental Organization forwarded to the president its recommendations for organizational changes in the Pentagon. In the Pentagon itself, Secretary McElroy had set up a distinguished advisory group on organizational matters headed by Charles A. Coolidge. As a result of these efforts the president became involved and spent many hours working on the details of reorganization plans. On one occasion, in January 1958, he met with the Coolidge group in the Pentagon. McElroy raised the question of whether the chairman should be given more power, and whether the members of the JCS should be separated from their service assignment as chiefs of staff. Radford, retired and a member of the group, thought the chairman needed no additional powers, since his real power came from his rapport with the secretary of defense. Omar Bradley agreed with Radford's conclusion. He felt, however, that the chairman's power came from his leadership and personal involvement with the chiefs.[45]

At this point the president, who thought the participants were too eager to support the status quo, interjected some thoughts of his own. He felt the public criticism of the department could not be brushed off. Further, he felt the group was talking about details rather than basic issues. He did not doubt that broad plans and estimates could be worked out harmoniously. When the issues involved specifics of men and money, however, it was hard to get an agreement that would hold up without certain people attacking it. Eisenhower said the defense secretary should take the stand that the primary duty of the chiefs was their JCS role. "Their greatest task was to work corporately in support of the president and secretary of defense." As for the service secretaries, the president felt they "should not be interested in matters of strategic planning." All in all McElroy's group was, Eisenhower thought, concentrating on "details rather than basic issues." He was determined not to gloss over the issues.[46]

The president was well aware of the spectrum of problems he would face in Congress in connection with his reorganization ideas.[47] First, there would be those trying to prod him into premature action, that is, to cause him to announce his proposals before he had developed in the Pentagon enough of a consensus to guarantee the military's subsequent support of the proposals before Congress. To secure that kind of bureaucratic consensus would take a little time.

An example of a congressional prod is a press release by Lyndon Johnson's Preparedness Subcommittee on January 27, 1958, which took an urgent attitude toward the need for defense reorganization. Another kind of problem came from members of the House Armed Services Committee, who felt their controls over defense matters were threatened. This is illustrated by a bill introduced into the House by Chairman Carl Vinson and others in late February 1958. This bill (H.R. 11001) was designed to reorganize in the opposite direction from that desired by the president. In effect, this bill would have weakened rather than strengthened the Defense Department and would have increased the power of the separate services.

On April 3, 1958, the president submitted a special message to Congress which contained his proposals for reorganization of the Defense Department.[48] These included the actions he would take as president and legislative actions that he was requesting of Congress. In the first category were the establishment of unified commands in the field under the secretary of defense, who would operate them through the JCS; the strengthening of the authority of the secretary of defense over the budget; and the elimination of the committee system employed by the Joint Staff, thus making it a truly operational staff. Legislative actions recommended included repeal of any statutory authority that vested responsibility for military operations in any official other than the secretary of defense; changing of the existing law to make it clear that each military chief could delegate major responsibilities to his vice chief; action by Congress to make appropriations for the Department of Defense in such a way as to provide the secretary with greater authority and flexibility; and elimination of the existing provisions for separate administration of the military departments and other similar restraints on the authority of the secretary of defense.

The Pentagon consensus on the president's proposals had not been completely achieved by the time of his message to Congress. Less than a week after the message Eisenhower met one evening with Secretary of Navy Gates and Chief of Naval Operations Burke, who had some apprehensions. Though they themselves completely accepted the concept of unified strategic planning, including placing all activities under control of the secretary of defense, they were concerned about others who felt differently.[49] They were particularly concerned about the naval staff in the Pentagon, where there was a great deal of "emotionalism and apprehension" over the reorganization. They also mentioned their "apprehensions over what might be done under some future president." In particular, they did not like that part of the proposal that eliminated the provision for the services to be "separately administered."

The discussion apparently did not clear up all Burke's misgivings or relieve the pressures on him from within the navy. Later, when he testified before the Senate Armed Services Committee, he opposed increasing the powers of the defense secretary and downgrading the status of the service secretaries. Twining subsequently discussed Burke's testimony with the president.[50] He indicated McElroy had read in full Burke's testimony on defense reorganization. McElroy, Twining said, felt that Burke had done well, but he had not gone "down the line" as some of the others had done.

The president followed up his message by submitting to Congress on April 16 a draft reorganization bill. The bill left out one important part of the message: the provision that gave the secretary of defense authority and flexibility in handling military appropriations. This proposal had upset Congress enough that it seemed best to delete it in the interest of the overall reorganization project. The president's commitment to the remainder of the legislation, however, was so great that he wrote directly to influential citizens all over the country asking them to contact the Congress in support of the proposed legislation.[51]

The day before he was to testify before the House committee on defense reorganization. McElroy called on the president. He wanted to hear Eisenhower's opinion as to how far the chiefs should go in their testimony.[52] The president indicated that if anyone gratuitously were to oppose his proposal, then that official "should be out." If a chief of staff, in responding to a committee question for his personal view, were to oppose some feature of the president's proposal, there would be no action against him, providing that subsequently he could loyally and faithfully execute the president's decisions. McElroy indicated that he understood Chairman Vinson planned to ask him for assurances that officers who testified against the proposal would not be penalized. On second thought, McElroy felt, he probably would not accept Vinson's question in those terms, since it was "inconsistent with the dignity of his office."

The struggle with Congress over the reorganization went on throughout the spring and early summer, but in the end the president got almost all he wanted. There were two points in the final bill that bothered him. First, Congress had sixty days in which to vote down any presidential proposal to transfer, merge, reassign, or abolish a "major combatant function." The other provision was one he referred to as "legalized insubordination." It permitted any member of the Joint Chiefs to define what constituted a "major function" and therefore to put into the congressional forum any proposed change by the president. It also gave the secretaries and chiefs the right to go directly to the Congress with any recommendations they deemed proper. In effect, then, the Reorganization Act of 1958 retained the separate military departments and with them sufficient alternative viewpoints that Congress would retain whatever meaningful control it still had in national security matters.[53]

In his memoirs, Dwight Eisenhower expresses himself very strongly with regard to his intent to get a balanced budget in fiscal year 1960.

> I planned to let the Congress know that if it materially added to the budget, I would respond with a veto, and that if the veto were overridden I would propose a tax increase to cover the increase in spending, and if necessary call a special session for the purpose.
>
> In preparing the budget, the giant military demands gave us, as usual, the gigantic headaches. No major item budgeted in each of the Armed Services was approved for inclusion unless the question "why" was answered to my satisfaction.[54]

After six years in office, and with the Congress heavily controlled by the Democrats, Eisenhower was well aware of the need for carefully thought-out legislative tactics. Apropos of this, an informal body of rules had been developed by this point to guide executive leaders appearing before congressional committees. These were designed to convey the impression of a united administration and to prevent executive personnel from providing gratuitous information to Congress. No testimony was allowed on matters under consideration by the administration but not yet resolved or released; how particular determinations had been reached by the administration; and specific advice that had been given the president.[55]

Another legislative approach frequently used by Eisenhower was meetings with congressional leadership, and at times with individual congressmen. One such meeting was with that perennial activist in defense matters, Senator Stuart Symington. Symington was subsequently prominent in the "missile gap" debate, as he had been in the earlier "bomber gap" controversy. In August 1958, however, when he met with the president, the administration seemed to have the missile situation under control. The purpose of the meeting, from the president's point of view, was to head off legislative problems. Symington had sent the president a letter stating that the United States was lagging behind the Soviets in missiles and alleged that the CIA had not accurately estimated the danger. Symington indicated, in his meeting with the president, that he had met with Allen Dulles (CIA director), and they had not been able to resolve their differences. The president said he had been through the matter a few days earlier, and he thought the CIA information on Soviet capabilities was "quite good." He felt that the problem was in future projections, allowing that different assumptions could cause widely different projections. As for U.S. programs, the president felt that it would be a mistake to rush production at the expense of development. Such reasoning was not likely to head off Stuart Symington, however. Both he and John Kennedy were to remain problems from the president's point of view by putting forth what Eisenhower considered to be "distorted statements and virulent attacks" on the adequacy of the Defense Department programs.[56]

In late November a meeting was held in the president's office to brief him on the status of the defense budget for fiscal 1960. Attendance included McElroy, Twining, Maurice Stans (the director of the budget), and about eight others from the White House and Defense Department staffs.[57] McElroy was the briefer, and he covered what he considered to be the key decisions. These were, in the main, force modernization issues. When the issue of navy carriers was reached, a protracted discussion ensued. Twining, in supporting the carrier program, pointed out their utility in cold war situations, while agreeing they were not of great value in general war. At that point Gordon Gray, then special assistant for national security affairs, interjected a comment on behalf of the absent Dulles. The secretary of state felt that the carriers recently used in Lebanon and Taiwan had been vital to those situations. He felt that as long as the United States retained the deterrent, the major threat was not general war but local aggression. He therefore wanted to express the thought that budget decisions should not be made that would cripple capabilities for local wars. McElroy pointed out that in Lebanon the United States had employed four carriers, and in Taiwan, five.

The president had some reservations. He did not visualize any battle for the surface of the sea. He then launched into a discussion of fiscal soundness, concluding that without fiscal soundness there was no defense. Eventually he deferred the immediate decision of whether or not to build a second nuclear carrier for another year.

Discussion of other hardware items was followed by comments on the overall defense budget. The president emphasized that defense was the key to a balanced budget, and unless the budget was balanced, "procurement of defense systems will avail nothing." McElroy defended his proposals by highlighting the risks already taken—for example, the downgrading of continental defense. The president raised the question of a possible reduction of ground forces in Europe. Twining agreed on the desirability of this, but felt the State Department should be consulted before pursuing the matter further.

After McElroy completed presenting the Defense Department's

views, Budget Director Maurice Stans had some remarks of his own. Although he agreed that the Defense Department had made substantial reductions, he felt more reductions were needed. There were still "exotic and duplicatory programs" included in the budget. As a result of his study of the matter, Stans felt he "could not recommend approval of the budget as presented by the defense department." His recommendation was either to use $40 billion as a ceiling or make up a new budget. McElroy again defended the budget on the basis of conscious risks already taken. In the end McElroy was asked to look over the budget again with a view toward further reductions. The NSC meeting at which this matter was to be taken up was set back to December 6 to give the defense staffs additional time. It was then agreed that a stag dinner for this group and others would provide an opportunity to discuss philosophy.

Following the dinner on the evening of December 3, the rather substantial number of guests moved to the White House library where a general discussion of economic considerations took place.[58] The president then asked each of the military chiefs to express his views. Taylor questioned the division of funds among the services, which failed to take into account army modernization requirements. He added that he felt it was "outside of his responsibility" to deal with the broad issue of a sound economy. The president contested this point, in effect stating that the industrial base and the economy have military significance. Burke stressed that if the competition between the United States and the Soviet Union required additional taxes they should be "generated." White felt that the ongoing reorganization of the Defense Department would result, over time, in savings by eliminating duplication. Twining said the United States had the big deterrent and forces enough to meet limited aggression of the Korean or Lebanese type. He also felt the important thing was to be decisive in using what was available when a crisis occurred. However, added Twining, if three or four crises happened simultaneously, the United States would be in "the big one." With that, school was out.

The day following the dinner, McElroy referred the revised defense budget to the Joint Chiefs as a corporate body for the first time. In the two days remaining before the NSC meeting of December 6, the chiefs were unable to agree on the budget. It was presented at that meeting, therefore, only with the endorsement of the chairman. For the upcoming congressional hearings, McElroy felt the need for some kind of written endorsement by the chiefs of the 1960 defense budget. He finally received a qualified endorsement in the form of a memorandum to him. The qualification was that each chief had "reservations with respect to the funding of their respective service programs."[59]

It might be well at this point to recapitulate these reservations by highlighting those programs which each service chief felt were inadequately supported in the administration's fiscal 1960 budget. The army's reservations were four: 1) Modernization of the existing army inventory would require $2.8 billion for each of the next five years—the administration was providing less than half of that in the budget year being considered; 2) the military personnel strength required to support army's worldwide requirements, especially for providing an adequate limited-war capability, was 925,000; the administration was providing for 870,000. A similar shortfall existed in Army Reserve Forces; 3) the army's surface-to-air missile program, Nike-Hercules, was not being adequately funded. This was designed to cope with the potential enemy bomber threat to the United States and areas overseas that were of strategic concern; and 4) the administration would provide only marginal research funds to support the army's proposed antimissile missile, the Nike-Zeus. The army wanted enough funds for intensive research, which, if successful, would lead to early production of the weapon.

The navy, for its part, had three major reservations: 1) There were inadequate funds for sustaining the fleet at what the navy leaders perceived to be the minimum level of slightly over 850 ships. The future was particularly troublesome in view of inadequate funds for procurement of ships, especially carriers; 2) there were inadequate funds for procuring Polaris submarines which the navy felt should take over a major part of the strategic missile mission; and 3) there were inadequate funds for the antisubmarine program which the navy leaders felt was moving too slowly.

The air force, which held the favored position in the proposed budget, was less critical than the other services, but it also had some reservations: 1) The aircraft of strategic bomber force were not being modernized rapidly enough. The air force, at least at chief of staff level, did not feel that the fiscal 1960 strategic missile program was inadequate; and 2) the Bomarc air defense missile was not being sufficiently funded.

Since funds were seen as inadequate, each service judged more could be obtained within the overall budget ceiling by curtailing certain programs of the other services. For example, the army felt that the air force's strategic retaliatory force was excessive in size. The navy agreed with this, but also felt the army did not need the increased personnel strength that it wanted over the budget allocation. The air force, not wanting any encroachments on its portion of the budget, agreed with the navy about army strength, but also resisted the navy's Polaris program. There were many other areas of mutual concern, such as the army's feeling that the air force was providing inadequate strategic air mobility to them, but the foregoing sets the stage for the public discussions of the fiscal 1960 budget.

The public presentation of the fiscal 1960 budget began with the State of the Union message on January 9, 1959. The following excerpt illustrates the president's use of his personal prestige: "The defense budget for the coming year has been planned on the basis of these principles and considerations. Over these many months I have personally participated in its development." Less than a week later, the president met with the congressional leaders of both parties to attempt to gain support for the budget. He also wrote hundreds of people to elicit their support in persuading Congress to adhere to the balanced budget he had developed.[60]

As for the budget itself, the defense portion was not much

greater than that of the year before. New obligational authority was set at $40.85 billion, with the same percentage breakdowns among the services that had held since the 1955 budget: air force, 46 percent; navy, 27 percent; and army, 23 percent. Strategic air power was again stressed at the expense of limited-war capability and both the army and navy modernization programs were held back to some extent.

By 1959 the climate was right for Congress to try to intervene more fully in defense matters. Technology was in a state of flux, providing many technical and strategic questions, and few people seemed certain of the answers. The goals of the services were sufficiently far apart so that it was not difficult to find points of conflict between services or between a service and the administration. The political climate caused by the congressional election just passed and the presidential one on the horizon also encouraged Congress to take on the administration. Finally, the top civilian leaders in the Pentagon were relatively new and inexperienced, whereas the opposite was true of congressional leaders interested in defense matters.[61]

Although congressional hearings and floor debates on the fiscal 1960 budget covered a multitude of issues, they focused particularly on three areas: the manner in which the executive branch had developed the defense budget, the adequacy of the defense budget, and the adequacy of U.S. limited-war capabilities.

When hearings began in the House, Defense Appropriations Chairman Mahon wanted to know what part McElroy had played in the formulation of the defense budget. McElroy stressed his personal role in the development, along with his deputy, Quarles, and the comptroller, McNeil. Initial expenditure figures were chosen at a slightly higher level than the previous year, and force levels were selected that were the same. This guidance was adequate until November, when the detailed work by the secretary of defense began, with conferences with each of the service secretaries and chiefs. Congressman John Riley wanted to know whether anyone else had given the secretary budgetary limits to use in his meetings with the services. He had in mind the direc-

tor of the Bureau of the Budget. McElroy denied that any such
guidance had been received. In the meetings with each service,
Riley asked, was there an opportunity for comment by one service on certain programs of the others? Not in those particular
meetings, answered the secretary, but the Joint Chiefs as a corporate body could do that.[62]

Chairman Twining, who testified with McElroy, was asked by
Mahon just what the role of the Joint Chiefs of Staff had been
in developing the budget. He indicated, without providing details, that the chiefs had had an opportunity to look it over as a
corporate body. Congressman Robert Sikes wanted to go back
one step to the formulation of the guidelines; did the chiefs have
a hand in developing those, he queried.[63] McElroy indicated that
they were not involved in the breakdown of dollars to the services. Sikes then asked Twining if the chiefs had participated in
formulating some kind of military, as contrasted with financial,
guidance from which the budget was developed. The question
was never explicitly answered, but it was obvious from the response that the answer was no.

Congressman Daniel Flood was interested in certain aspects of
the president's role in developing the budget and led up to it by
discussing economic considerations. "Is there such a thing . . . as
an arbitrary demarcation dollar line at Defense because our economy cannot stand it," he asked McElroy.[64] McElroy answered
that there had been none in the preparation of the budget. Flood
was skeptical and felt that if such a notion of an arbitrary ceiling
for defense existed he would attack it "bitterly." Did McElroy
have any instructions from the president that he must maintain
his budget at about the present level for several years? The secretary denied this and went on to say that there was no feeling on
the president's part that national security was to be subordinated
to the budget.

When General Taylor testified along with Army Secretary
Brucker, the question of the role of the Joint Chiefs in budget
formulation was surfaced several times, and Taylor did his best
to clear up the matter. In the process he also cleared up Twin-

ing's rather misleading answer. The JCS as a corporate body participated in budget development only as much as the secretary of defense wanted them to participate, said Taylor.[65] The budget now under consideration had been given to the Joint Chiefs one evening and was to be presented less than two days later to the NSC. This, he indicated, was not an adequate amount of time to study the overall defense budget.

Admiral Burke and Navy Secretary Gates testified the week following the army leaders. Congressman Charles Boyle said he had problems understanding just what the role of the service secretary was in budget matters.[66] Gates pointed out that he worked for the president and agreed with his fiscal and security policies. However, he said, this would not prevent him from being completely frank with Congress in setting forth his own beliefs when requested. Boyle allowed that the reason he had asked the question was an impression he had that perhaps some important information concerning the formulation of the defense budget was being withheld from the committee. Gates assured him this was not so.

General White, the air force chief of staff, who testified along with Secretary Douglas, was asked by Congressman Jamie Whitten whether White would ask the committee for increased funds if he disagreed with the executive budget as developed.[67] White thought that would be inappropriate, and if he felt that strongly about some matter he would not appear as air force chief of staff. However, he would certainly provide his personal views on questions specifically directed to him by the committee, whether they agreed with the administration or not.

Congressional probing and the obvious attempts by Congress to exploit differences within the administration did not go unnoticed in the White House. In early February, Chairman Twining met with the president in the Oval Office to discuss a number of defense matters.[68] Twining mentioned that during the House hearings Congress had exhibited some sensitivity toward their prerogatives of raising and maintaining "armies." The problem arose over personnel strengths of the army, marines, and reserve components. The secretary of defense had been questioned extensively concerning the increment of strength that many in Congress thought should be added to the administration's program. The conversation then turned to motives of individual congressmen in "interfering" with the administration's force structure program. The president was not too concerned with the immediate problem and felt he could handle the matter of strengths.

Each of the major officials who testified during the House hearings was queried on the adequacy of the defense budget. Mahon's questioning of McElroy was direct and to the point.

Q. Mr. Secretary, did you think that the military budget as presented to the Congress is adequate for the United States?

A. Yes, sir.

Q. Are there any significant weaknesses which you think are inherent in the 1960 defense budget before us, any major weaknesses?

A. No, sir.

Later on, Congressman W. F. Norrell took a different approach with McElroy. If McElroy were president, Norrell queried, would this be the budget he would recommend? McElroy replied affirmatively. General Twining also supported the budget as being adequate, although he acknowledged that the services had some reservations on their particular programs.[69]

When the army leaders were queried on the adequacy of the budget, the response was quite different. Not only did General Taylor indicate that certain army programs were not adequately funded, but he felt certain other programs were being funded in a manner excessive to military requirements. While satisfied with the overall budget, he felt the internal allocation was incorrect. Under questioning, he indicated that he had in mind strategic weapons. He felt the funding for both the strategic weapons and the strategic weapons systems was above what was militarily required.[70]

Gates and Burke both felt that the overall budget was adequate. Had they been in charge of allocating it among the services, however, they would have done it differently. What Burke had in mind, he implied, was an excess of strategic weapons in the air force. The navy needed some new ships, aircraft, some ship rehabilitation, and finally, funding for an additional new Polaris.[71]

The air force leaders were asked by Chairman Mahon their views on the overall adequacy of the budget itself and its allocation among the services. Douglas and White agreed as to the overall adequacy. Both allowed that there were certain air force programs on which some hard decisions had to be made. The air force proportion (46 percent) of the defense budget, however, they thought was about right.[72]

The question of the United States' capability to engage in limited war was brought up by the committee with each of the major witnesses. Both McElroy and Twining indicated that U.S. resources were adequate for limited war. They were challenged on this with quotations from a recent speech by Taylor, which had highlighted what he felt were inadequacies in the areas of strategic mobility, modernization, and personnel strength of the army. At times the dialogue became heated, but McElroy and Twining held their ground. The latter emphasized that the other chiefs disagreed with Taylor on particulars such as airlift adequacy.[73]

The army's presentation put heavy emphasis on limited war as the most likely form of aggression. Sikes, a general in the army reserves, presented Taylor with some excellent questions by which Taylor could develop his limited-war views. Sikes wanted to know if the fiscal 1959 budget had reduced the army's limited-war capability. Taylor indicated it had and that fiscal 1960 allowed no improvement. Mahon wanted to know which wars the United States would have deterred if there had been additional limited-war capability. In view of subsequent events, the portion of his answer pertaining to Indochina is interesting. Taylor opined, "We could have gone into the Indochina War and probably should have." [74]

Arleigh Burke felt that the U.S. capability for limited war had increased only slightly in recent years, while the capability for general war had been significantly increased during the same period. However, Gates felt that the United States was, nevertheless, in a position to handle limited war if it came.[75]

The air force's presentation stated that the United States' capability of waging a limited war was good. Great stress was placed on allied forces that, together with U.S. forces, presented local aggressors with a "formidable obstacle." Congressman Norrell asked White about U.S. capabilities for limited and general war, and their relative importance. White's answer was: "I think we will have the forces to do both in the degree necessary, sir. As to the relative importance, I think there can be no doubt that the general war is the most dangerous."[76]

By the time defense appropriations hearings began in the Senate in May, the headlines were gone, but the issues remained. McElroy's opening statement acknowledged the ongoing debate on defense matters. There were divergent opinions on many issues, he said, but still specific programs must be developed. The central problem, he felt, was one of achieving balance between forces for general war and limited war. All views could not be satisfied; hence the problem was one of making hard choices, so as to avoid dissipation of U.S. resources. Anticipating questions on the adequacy of the budget, McElroy included a discussion on that issue in his prepared statement based on the chiefs' paper of January 19. This was the paper in which each had stated that the budget was adequate in an overall sense, yet each had reservations about his own program.[77]

One problem that particularly bothered the subcommittee was the question of who set the strength of the military services, the executive or Congress. The Senate had recently passed a supplemental bill to the 1959 defense budget in which it had provided that the army should not be reduced to fewer than 900,000 personnel, and the marines to not fewer than 200,000. The Defense Department, however, was busily engaged in reducing to 875,000 and 175,000 respectively. In the event that the bill cleared both houses with the mandatory language, Senator Dennis Chavez wondered what the administration would do. McElroy was not in a mood to back down on this one: "Both the President and I would view with considerable gravity the tendency on the part of . . . the legislative body of the United States to put rigidity into the defense budget and program."[78]

For some reason McElroy did not have the same concern about congressional intrusion into issues involving competing weapons systems. In what became one of his most quoted statements, he indicated that the Defense Department had not done too well in solving the Bomarc-Nike controversy. Further, he indicated that it would not bother him if Congress "held our feet to the fire" on that issue. Later, Defense Comptroller Wilfred McNeil interpreted this to mean not that Congress should make a decision for defense on the controversy, but rather that they should "keep the pressure on us." The day after McNeil's statement, the subcommittee received a letter from McElroy in a further attempt at clarifying his politically awkward statement. What he meant was that it would not be disturbing if Congress pressed for a "master plan" from the administration, which would, of course, include a requirement for both Bomarc and Nike.[79]

When Army Secretary Wilber Brucker and Vice Chief Lyman Lemnitzer appeared, Symington queried them on the adequacy of the army budget. Did Secretary Brucker think Taylor was right in being dissatisfied with his share of the budget, or was Chairman Twining, who was satisfied with the budget, right? Symington did not get the question answered, but the army's reservations on the budget were placed in the record.[80]

Symington also questioned Gates and Vice Chief J. S. Russell on their reservations. Russell answered the question by listing five areas in which the navy, "if the national economy would permit," would like to apply more dollars. Symington pointed out that the USSR was spending as much as the United States on defense, with only half the gross national product. At this stage of the hearings he got no takers on that, and the discussion returned to more technical matters. As Russell continued his testimony, he made a rather strong case for the Polaris and seemed to question the effectiveness of fixed overseas bases. Senator Henry Dworshak thought that Russell was, perhaps unintentionally, disparaging the air force in his attempt to build the navy's case. As the dialogue continued, Russell told Dworshak that he thought the senator was unduly sensitive and that he, Russell, was present to defend the navy budget, not the air force budget.[81]

When Air Force Secretary Douglas and Chief of Staff White appeared, the routine question on reservations brought forth a routine reply stressing a need for more rapid replacement of the B-47, acceleration of Bomarc, more money for construction and for operations and maintenance. The questioning became more exciting when Symington asked White his views on the "over-kill" theory. Symington pointed out that both Taylor and Burke had testified that the U.S. retaliatory capability was greater than required; this implied that some of the budgetary emphasis should be shifted toward items that the army and navy felt required greater attention. White disagreed categorically with Taylor and Burke, both with regard to "the philosophy which underlies their statements . . . [and] the quantitative forces . . . involved."[82] White went on to develop his case, central to which was the desirability of attacking the enemy's military strength, not just cities and industry.

Floor debate took place in the House on June 2 and 3, 1959. Aside from the usual trivial or parochial issues, the debate concerned three major areas: strategic defensive forces, exemplified by the debate concerning the air force's Bomarc against the army's Nike-Hercules, and a more visionary development, the army's Nike-Zeus; strategic offensive forces, especially the so-called missile gap; and limited-war forces. This latter category included army and marine strength; modernization of all forces, especially the army; airlift; and a new carrier for the navy. The latter item was particularly salient and had become largely, but not exclusively, identified with its limited-war role, rather than its retaliatory role. During the House debate, amendments to raise army strength were defeated, although some funds were added for modernization. The House also supported its committee's action in dropping a proposed carrier from the administration's budget, with the bulk of the saved funds going into antisubmarine warfare. One of the more far-ranging statements in the Senate debate was that by Lyndon Johnson, in which he used the issue of the "missile gap" and other alleged inadequacies to attack the administration's defense policies and posture. The Bureau of the Budget served as the whipping boy. Senator John Carroll thought the fact that Congress could appropriate additional funds, but that the administration, acting through the Budget Bureau, could prevent the Defense Department from spending them, constituted "amazing revelations." [83] This discussion took place in the context of how the Congress could force the administration to comply with a 200,000 personnel floor for the marine corps, and how it could be assured that funds appropriated for modernizing the army would not, in fact, be used for something else. In the end it was concluded that the most Congress could do, by way of appropriation, was to provide that the personnel strength be maintained and that the funds provided for both items would not be used elsewhere.

On the second day of debate, Lyndon Johnson was in rare form. He was particularly rankled about some errors in estimates. He thought an old adversary, the Bureau of Budget, was to blame. He called upon the director of the bureau immediately to review testimony during the hearings and to provide Congress with corrected estimates. He felt Congress was being placed in a "false light" by the administration using "hide and seek financing" to cover deficiencies and supplemental requirements while at the same time accusing Congress of "budget busting." [84]

Later Johnson, in an exchange with Republican Senator Leverett Saltonstall concerning the president's desires on a nuclear carrier, was rather pointed. Was Saltonstall, in agreeing to a nuclear carrier, disagreeing with "his leader"? Saltonstall retorted, "I would never disagree with my leader, publicly at least." Johnson replied, "I wish we could put the Democrats in a straitjacket like that." [85]

Final action took place in both houses on August 4. The final bill was about $20 million less than the administration's request. There were many internal changes, but none was dramatic. For example, a nuclear carrier was funded, but only enough to begin work. Both the president's strategic policy and his budgetary ceiling, by whatever name, remained intact.

An examination of the congressional phase of the fiscal 1960 defense budget indicates that participation by Congress was piecemeal. Issues were examined without any particular attempt to interrelate them with each other or to the defense budget as a whole. There appears to have been little examination of the underlying rationale of the defense budget or any kind of systematic approach to reviewing it. Considering Eisenhower's determination to balance his budget, his skill in managing the budgetary process, the public's confidence in his military judgment, and the relatively short time and limited resources available to Congress for examining the defense budget, perhaps the outcome is not surprising. Eisenhower's strategic policy and his defense budget ceiling remained intact. What Congress provided was rhetoric and some headlines; their effect on defense policy or budget was negligible.[86]

While the fiscal 1960 defense budget was being developed, there arose a challenge to the Eisenhower strategy that was perceived as being of crisis proportions, at least for a time. The challenge began with Khrushchev's announcement on November 10, 1958, that the USSR would sign a peace treaty with East Germany that would terminate allied rights in Berlin. On November 27 this was rephrased into the form of an ultimatum, addressed to the occupation powers and the Federal Republic, and setting a six months' deadline, by which time negotiations over the future of Berlin had to be productive. The main point of the note was the proposition that West Berlin become a "free city." In effect, the Western states had until May 27, 1959, to negotiate an agreement over Berlin. The note also included a threat to disrupt access to the city and warned that aggressive action against any member of the Warsaw Pact would be cause for appropriate retaliation.[87]

What were the motives of the Soviet leadership in initiating this offensive? One explanation was to get the allies out of Berlin and to achieve a peace treaty at least with East Germany. This would weaken the American and NATO positions relative to the Soviet Union.[88]

Another explanation was that the action was in response to the United States' decision to deploy IRBMs to Europe. Perhaps Khrushchev was afraid that the NATO decision of December 1957 which facilitated these deployments would allow West Germany to gain access to nuclear weapons. The crisis, according to this explanation, was intended to persuade the United States to reverse its plan and perhaps eventually to accede to a nuclear-free zone in Europe.[89] On the other hand, perhaps all Khrushchev was seeking was a summit conference to settle certain outstanding issues. Whatever the explanation for the Soviet action, the confrontation over Berlin developed a life of its own and became in effect a cold war test of wills between the United States and the Soviet Union.

On December 11, immediately following a routine NSC meeting, the president met in his office with the vice president and about a dozen other officials. The purpose of the meeting was to discuss contingency plans in event of closure of the Berlin corridors to the allies. The president asked State Department representatives, headed by Christian Herter, their views on the use of token force to gain access to the city. Their response was that the key issue was U.S. willingness to employ force in the first instance; that would be the greatest deterrent. General Taylor then proceeded to outline the JCS position, which was first to verify that attempts to use the corridors had in fact been stopped by force.[90] This would then lead to a choice between two alternatives: the use of airlift, which the JCS felt was "a form of defeat," or the use of more force. One presidential aide felt that the major problem was how to get the USSR to use force first. Taylor pointed out that if a convoy were stopped it would not remain at the

detention point but would leave. He again reiterated his disin-
clination "to retreat to the use of airlift." The president felt, in
closing the meeting, that the notion of causing the other side to
use force should be discussed soon with the British, to allow them
maximum time for consideration, since he felt there might be difficulties with them on this issue.[91]

The North Atlantic Council subsequently considered the Berlin situation in its December meeting and issued a declaration
that indicated, along with support for the three Western occupy-
ing powers, that NATO would not approve any solution which
did not "assure freedom of communication between that city and
the free world." About the end of December, Washington, London, Paris, and Bonn replied to the Soviet note of November 27.
In their replies the allies indicated that Berlin must be discussed
in a broader context, rejected the idea of negotiations under a
deadline, and stressed an interest in negotiations. On January 10,
1959, the Soviets responded with a note that included a draft
peace treaty for Germany. It is doubtful whether anyone took
the proposed peace treaty at face value, but it seemed at first to
indicate a willingness to broaden the base of discussion. A subsequent press release from Tass, however, contradicted the impression of any relenting on the Berlin issue.[92]

In late January there was a meeting in the president's office on
Berlin developments with state and defense officials. A disagreement developed between Dulles and the Joint Chiefs over the
amount of force to be applied if an American convoy were
stopped. The chiefs felt one division should be employed, whereas Dulles felt that allied opinion would not be sufficiently mobil-
ized at the outset to permit such a large force. The president
sided with Dulles, but for a different reason. He felt one division
had "insufficient capability to do an acceptable job" and was too
large for a show of force. General Twining at that point made a
strong presentation of the Joint Chiefs' position.[93] The president
countered with the dangers of taking unilateral action. He felt
Konrad Adenauer would not go along with a "Berlin or bust"
situation. Dulles reaffirmed his willingness to risk war when nec-

essary, but he felt the first obstruction to movement would not be sufficient reason to take such a risk. He felt there would be ample time to send a division after pausing to consider the move.

There followed a discussion of allied ground capabilities in Europe. Twining pointed out that U.S. strategic policy precluded a limited war in Europe, and since there were insufficient means to fight the USSR in a conventional war, the United States "must be prepared to fight a general nuclear war." The president expressed the opinion that the Soviets would not, when the time came, counter Western application of token force. He agreed that the United States had insufficient forces in Europe to fight a conventional war. If the Soviets used military force, he said, the allies would be in a position to issue an ultimatum prior to initiation of general war. In the end the plan agreed upon was to apply minimum force before making a decision on the employment of larger allied forces.

In mid-February the Western powers replied to the Soviet note of January 10. The key point was a proposal for a foreign ministers' conference to discuss the overall German problem. At a press conference at about the same time, the president was asked if there was an allied agreement to use force, if necessary, to defend rights in Berlin. The president avoided answering the question directly, stating it could only be answered in the context of a particular situation. In his next news conference, later in the month, in answer to a question concerning the strategy for defending allied rights in Berlin, the president made a vague reference to NATO plans. In a news conference on March 11, the president was asked, "Is the United States prepared to use nuclear war if necessary to defend free Berlin?" His answer was equivocal, but later in the same conference he indicated that a ground war would place the United States at a disadvantage. Still later in the conference he said, "I didn't say that nuclear war is a complete impossibility." [94]

Meanwhile, Dulles had completed his last journey as secretary of state to London, Paris, and Bonn, attempting to get some kind of East-West negotiation over Berlin under way. Prime Minister

Harold Macmillan was preparing for his own trip to Moscow when Dulles arrived in London. Macmillan's views on dealing with the Soviet Union were quite flexible, and he was anxious to get agreement on an early East-West conference. As for employing force on the ground in the Berlin corridors, Macmillan was opposed. Instead, he favored resorting to an airlift if necessary.[95]

Charles de Gaulle opposed any conference before the May 27 deadline, but did agree with the British preference for an airlift. Later, when Macmillan visited de Gaulle after visiting Moscow, the question of the danger of war came up. De Gaulle said, "Je ne peux pas faire la guerre—on ne me donne pas les bombes atomiques!"[96] I would translate this to mean that for a nation that does not have atomic weapons there is not much use talking about preparations for war.

Dulles's final stop was to see Adenauer who, while skeptical, went along with the idea of negotiations before the deadline of the Soviet ultimatum. He too preferred airlift to a ground probe in developing contingency plans. It was shortly after Dulles's return that the mid-February note to the USSR was sent. It was answered by the Soviets in a note of March 2, in which they agreed to a foreign ministers' conference for purposes of discussing Berlin as well as a peace treaty and removed the ultimatum date of May 27.

On March 6 the president met twice with legislative groups over the concern in the country about the Berlin crisis.[97] His objective was to develop some common understanding between the two branches as pertained to Berlin. Several of the legislators expressed their concern over the adequacy of U.S. forces in a time of crisis. His response was similar to what he said to other critics such as Dean Acheson, who was at that time actively campaigning for more conventional power and less reliance on massive retaliation. This statement gives an excellent insight into Eisenhower's thinking on strategic policy.

Many people seemed to assume that . . . I should abandon my determination to enforce strict economy on defense expenditures. This showed a total lack of understanding of our military problem. If resort to arms should become necessary, our troops in Berlin would be quickly overrun, and the conflict would almost inevitably be global war. For this type of war our nuclear forces were more than adequate. . . . I determined that this crisis should not affect our long-range plans for assuring the defense of America without waste. Indeed, it was always my conviction that one purpose of Khrushchev's manufactured crisis was to frighten free populations and governments into unnecessary and debilitating spending sprees.[98]

Having had a reasonably successful session with the congressional leaders, the president felt it was now time to take the problem to the American people, which he did on the night of March 16 by radio and television.[99] His talk covered both the Berlin situation, stressing the need to stand firm, and the state of U.S. defenses. The latter part was designed to counter ongoing criticism of the U.S. defense program and to head off efforts in Congress to reduce the mutual security program.

Macmillan, having completed his trip to the Soviet Union and having visited with de Gaulle and Adenauer, headed for Washington and several days of meetings with Eisenhower, commencing on March 20 at Camp David. The meetings covered a wide range of subjects related to Berlin in particular, and Europe in general. Strategic matters at this point had been reduced to contingency planning for Berlin. At the opening meeting Macmillan asked what would happen if access to Berlin were interrupted. The president indicated that he would seek to open access, unless force were employed by the other side.[100]

At a meeting the following day Donald Quarles indicated that four kinds of plans were being studied: reopening access through local ground operations, airlift, naval actions, and the initiation of measures of general warfare. Selwyn Lloyd, the British foreign secretary, asked what would be done if local operations could not open access. Twining said that if force were used to block a substantial allied military force, that "would let us know that this is a major military operation." John Irwin, an assistant secretary of defense, said the use of substantial force would come after all political and other measures had been tried. Macmillan wrote in his diary of this discussion, "The American Defense people seemed much more realistic than they had been some months and weeks ago. I do not now fear that they will take (unless some generals get out of hand) any dangerous action." The following day the president said he had been giving some thought to what could be done short of war if the Soviets took action against the allies. What he had concluded, he indicated, was to stop trade, institute a blockade, or break off relations. This, he felt, was "contingency planning in the broadest sense."[101]

These meetings, which culminated in the decision to propose to the USSR a foreign ministers' meeting and later, if appropriate, a summit meeting, ended the first phase of the Berlin confrontation, the so-called deadline crisis. The overall Berlin confrontation was to go on until 1962, finally ending with the Cuban missile crisis in October of that year. It is ironic that John Kennedy, so critical of Eisenhower's strategic innovation, was to employ it as his centerpiece in terminating both the Cuban missile and the Berlin crises simultaneously.

By the summer of 1959, with the Berlin crisis out of the way for the moment and his fiscal 1960 defense budget through Congress, the president had to face the annual argument over the Basic National Security Paper. The meeting on this issue is interesting because it sums up the position of the Eisenhower administration on strategy as it moved toward the end of its term of office. There were no major changes in the remaining time of the administration.

The meeting was held in early July in the president's office; present were Christian Herter, now secretary of state; Neil McElroy and his new deputy, Thomas Gates; Arthur Radford, recalled to active duty temporarily for an ailing Nathan Twining; Gerard Smith; Gordon Gray; and Andrew Goodpaster. The basic issue was whether there was to be any change in the way the BNSP was worded. Herter introduced two familiar problem areas: what constitutes general war, and the U.S. capabilities for limited war.[102] Herter was concerned that the existing wording of the policy indicated that any hostilities between the United

States and the Soviet Union would automatically result in general war. The real issue, especially for the allies, he felt, was the assumption that nuclear weapons would be used automatically when U.S. forces were involved. McElroy felt the issue was whether the U.S. force structure should be based on the assumption that nuclear weapons would be used in limited war. The president said that the basic point was that the United States had to have nuclear weapons available wherever there were substantial U.S. forces.

McElroy commented that the army, navy, and marines felt there should be greater reliance on conventional forces in limited war situations. Radford recalled that beginning in 1953 the United States had built its forces on the assumption that atomic weapons would be available if needed. Radford stated that if there were any possibility of going to war without atomic weapons, the forces would be structured a great deal differently than they were. It would not be possible, he thought, to maintain forces of the size needed if they were limited to conventional weapons. The president felt there was a wide range of possibilities and that it was very difficult to find generalizations to cover that range.

McElroy pointed out that in any case it would be very difficult to change the language of the BNSP without this being interpreted as a significant change of policy. Not only would this increase the possibility of many other changes, but it might also cause the allies to question U.S. credibility. Gates said it should be understood that some people were in fact recommending a change in policy, on the basis that the need for conventional forces is more likely in a situation close to nuclear parity. Gray indicated his understanding was that the State Department was proposing that the United States should develop the capability to engage in limited operations without using atomic weapons. The president felt that this capability already existed. However, in areas of potential contact with Soviet or Chinese forces, the atomic capacity must be available.

Herter, reading from a State Department paper, then indicated that while nuclear weapons were adequate as a deterrent, they were not desirable for use in limited warfare, except as a last resort. The president felt this was too cautious and restrictive an approach. The president understood that excessive means should not be used to meet problems. He thought, however, that defense should continue to incorporate atomic weapons into the structure, but not preclude the possibility of using forces we had in a conventional role. In general, though, he felt that the atomic bridge had been crossed. "If we are attacked in Korea, for example, we are going to use atomic weapons." In this case he was referring to units on the Eurasian land mass. Units involved in areas remote from Soviet power were another matter. The meeting ended with the president questioning the validity of definitions of the type attempted in the BNSP.

In the various positions set forth in this meeting, there were three clusters of strategic concepts. The first of these was the strategic policy of the administration, of which the president was the chief proponent. His bureaucratic allies were the secretaries of the treasury and defense, and until about 1958 the secretary of state, as well as the chairman of the Joint Chiefs of Staff and the chief of staff of the air force. Although there were variations among the major figures in this cluster, their views may be summed up as follows. There was a definite limit on defense spending if the economy were to remain sound and able to support a true national security. This limit required setting priorities among the competing defense programs. The most disposable element was manpower, the least disposable elements were strategic retaliatory power and continental defense. War with the Soviet Union, or any war on the scale of Korea, would require the use of atomic weapons, probably from the outset. As war from the Soviet Union became remote, nonatomic solutions were possible. For these situations the conventional forces on hand were adequate.

The second cluster included the secretary of state from late 1958 onward and the navy leaders who, however, began to shift to the third cluster as time went on. The view of the second group was that there was a need to develop additional force capabilities for lesser wars. They also questioned the utility of tactical nuclear weapons in many situations. Dulles began to move in this direction in 1958, although he supported the need for tactical nuclear weapons. He was under pressure from within his department to adopt the more flexible approach characteristic of the second cluster. He also was concerned in the post-Sputnik period about the credibility of the New Look strategy in the eyes of the allies and with the American people themselves. While this concern might cause him to raise the issue with Eisenhower, he was not inclined to risk his power base with the president by openly moving into the second cluster, especially in forums at which the president was present. Perhaps when he expressed doubts about the existing policy he was merely organizing his ideas. On the other hand, perhaps he felt the price he would have to pay for taking a position approaching Taylor's would be too great for what would be gained. Herter's position also placed him in the second cluster. He had very definite concerns that any conflict between the United States and the Soviet Union would automatically involve nuclear weapons. Further, he felt that the use of tactical nuclear weapons in limited war was not desirable.

The third cluster of strategic concepts had, for a long time, only one major proponent—the army leaders. In time the navy leaders began to move openly in that direction, except that the navy did not envision the large manpower requirement for land forces visualized by the army. The most sophisticated articulation of the third cluster of concepts by a member of the administration was that of Maxwell Taylor. He wanted to recognize a limitation on the use of nuclear weapons at the outset of any conflict. Further, he would attempt to handle small wars entirely with conventional forces. Taylor also believed in finite deterrence, but as time went on, so did everyone else, except for the air force.

One aspect of his nuclear-heavy strategy on which Eisenhower continued to experience frustrations, while at the same time mak-

ing small gains, was the problem of nuclear sharing with the
NATO allies. Through his efforts Congress, for a second time,
liberalized the Atomic Energy Act in July 1958. Additional information concerning weapons systems could be provided to the
allies, although there was no relaxation in the requirement that
United States personnel would retain custody of the warheads.
As for weapons production, the 1958 amendments continued
what the 1954 act had permitted de facto—assistance to the British but not to the French.[103] Eventually the latter went their
own way and became the fourth nuclear power.

In the last full year of his administration President Eisenhower was still concerned whether we were "treating our Allies
properly" on this question. Sometimes he had some help from
the supreme allied commander in Europe—theoretically an international post, but in reality an American proconsul in Europe.
On the first page of the *New York Times* of March 3, 1960, there
was an article datelined Paris in which the opening paragraph
read: "Gen. Lauris Norstad, Supreme Allied Commander in
Europe, announced today that the United States, Britain and
France had tacitly agreed to integrate a battalion each into a
task force that would have atomic weapons." It was a nice try
but it never worked out that way.[104]

In his final summer in office Dwight Eisenhower was still
grappling with the desire by the European allies to have some
nuclear weapons under their own control. He held a series of
meetings with Chairman John McCone of the Atomic Energy
Commission, General Norstad, and Robert Bowie who had just
completed a study on the future of NATO. In the end the problem was never solved and continued on into the 1970s. "The difficulty," Eisenhower said, "was not with the Europeans but with
our own Congress, which strives to keep in its own hands details
of military policy and similar operations." He agreed with Norstad that there "was a need for the Europeans to have some control
of atomic warheads." He was not optimistic, however, about the
possibility, adding that "the Joint Committee on Atomic Energy
is unconstitutional in its functions." McCone added that he was

"not sanguine about breaking up the Joint Committee," since it was "too deeply entrenched."[105] In nuclear sharing President Eisenhower was never able to go as far as he wished, but this did not prevent continued allied acceptance of and dependence on his nuclear-heavy strategy.

Sputnik became an external stimulus to force modernization in the armed services, out of proportion to its military implications. The president took a more balanced view of the Soviet success than most, but he understood the psychological impact and supported force modernization where it seemed to be beneficial. He also understood the natural predilections of service representatives to exploit the situation by expanding both their qualitative and quantitative requirements for military hardware. He attempted to counter this trend, first, by advancing strategic arguments rather than becoming involved in detailed discussions of force requirements, and, second, by applying ad hoc budget ceilings and, at the same time, stressing the importance of not weakening the economy by excessive defense spending. It is evident that even after the spectacular psychological reaction of the public to Sputnik, Eisenhower's first consideration was the domestic economy and as modest a defense budget as he could get by with.

The New Look had been developed when the United States held a near monopoly on strategic weapons delivery systems. The NATO allies had accepted the New Look in their December 1954 meeting, under the assumption that U.S. territory was not vulnerable to Soviet strategic weapons. Sputnik changed allied assumptions about American invulnerability. Western European leaders no doubt asked themselves whether the New Look strategy was still credible under the new conditions. Specifically, would the American president risk his homeland in order to protect Western Europe in event of a confrontation with the USSR? In response, the U.S. leadership gave assurances by offering greater allied participation in the operational aspects of U.S. strategy, but did not offer any change in that strategy.

Likewise, the Berlin crisis did not change U.S. strategy. It did cause considerable thinking, however, about how that strategy was to be applied below the level of nuclear warfare. The best approach, said the president, was to apply minimum force and await developments. There would be time, he felt, to issue an ultimatum before escalating to general nuclear war, which he did not preclude. He did list, however, many less severe options of a nonmilitary nature, and he himself favored a gradual escalation, beginning with diplomatic means.

No doubt the sensitivities of the allied leaders conditioned Eisenhower's approach to applying his strategy. One thing seems certain, however: neither the piecemeal changes in Soviet capabilities brought about by Sputnik nor a passing crisis like Berlin was going to cause Dwight Eisenhower to change his strategic policy. As he said, those people who felt "he should abandon his determination . . . to enforce strict economy on defense expenditures . . . showed a total lack of understanding of our military problem." The domestic context, and not the external context, shaped strategic policy.

The fiscal 1959 budget was developed in circumstances just the reverse of the economizing mood of the previous year, because of what some people perceived as an extraordinary change in the external context. Nevertheless, to the president, holding down the defense budget was more important than the external context.

An examination of the development of the fiscal 1960 defense budget, in particular the congressional phase, indicates that congressional participation was piecemeal. Congressional impotence in this case seems partly related to the unique circumstances of the time, but, even more, it seems to be built into the system itself. Issues, in the main those on which the services expressed reservations, were examined without any particular attempt to interrelate them with one another or to the defense budget as a whole. There appears to have been little examination of the underlying rationale of the defense budget or any kind of systematic approach to reviewing it. Considering Eisenhower's determination to balance his budget, his skill in employing defense policy and budget processes, the public's confidence in his military judgment, and the relatively short time and limited resources available to Congress for examining the defense budget, the outcome is not surprising. Eisenhower's strategic policy and his defense budget ceiling remained intact.

In 1958, as in 1953, the president resorted to reorganization of the Defense Department as a means of gaining tighter control over the Pentagon. He understood the desirability of organizing in such a way as to have a forced agreement built into the system on the real issue, the budget. The goal would be a single military budget, controlled by the Defense Department. In effect, this would have abolished the service departments and with them the organized bureaucratic support of alternative defense policies. This was one of the few holds Congress had on defense matters, and it had no intention of relinquishing it.

The president's skepticism about doctrinal papers, such as the BNSP, is clearly expressed in the annual review of that document in the summer of 1959. At that meeting Eisenhower openly questioned the validity of attempting to define strategy with the precision that was attempted in the BNSP.[106] McElroy's comment, at the same meeting, about the difficulties that would be caused by rewording the paper is also revealing. He had two points: changing the wording would open the gate to other changes; and changes would lead to credibility problems with the allies. This implied that the wording of the document did not have an important effect on strategic policy; otherwise he would not have advanced either argument against making changes in the document.

Two final observations on the episodes seem justified. The primacy of Eisenhower as the shaper of strategic policy is evident. And the forum for strategic policy discussion and decision was the small meeting in the Oval Office, not the formal sessions of the NSC. Pertinent to the first observation, Eisenhower's aggressiveness and confidence in handling his strategic policy adversaries (such as Taylor and to a lesser extent Burke) is quite noticeable.

Apropos of the second observation, one cannot, without seeing the minutes of the NSC meetings, which I have not, speak with absolute certainty about that body. However, it does seem clear from the evidence that the Oval Office was where Eisenhower made the real strategic decisions.

*CHAPTER FOUR*

# Conclusions

THIS HAS BEEN a study of the making of strategic policy in the Eisenhower administration and, in some ways, of Eisenhower himself. The evidence examined, including public papers and commentary as well as discussion during private meetings, supports the view that Eisenhower provided very strong presidential leadership in achieving a strategic innovation in 1953–1954 and later defending it successfully against those who wanted it changed. It should not be surprising that Eisenhower felt confident in matters of strategic policy. His selection by George Marshall to command the allied forces in Europe was based on Marshall's reading not only of Eisenhower's personality but also of his skill as a strategic manager. Eisenhower's preparation in the 1930s had been sound, including six years as an immediate assistant to Douglas MacArthur. During World War II Eisenhower consorted with kings, presidents, and prime ministers; he was the embodiment of the allied victory in Europe. When Europe needed him again in 1950 he became the first supreme allied commander for NATO. Who had more reason to be confident in his ability to achieve a strategic innovation than Eisenhower? What is of more interest is how he managed to maintain his strategic innovation against increasingly strong opposition.

Eisenhower's major campaign promises in 1952, which were oriented toward the domestic context, had a significant influence on U.S. strategic policy when those promises were implemented. These promises were to liquidate the Korean War, to balance the budget, and to reduce taxes. Liquidation of the war did result in a reduced budget. Additional reductions in the budget were obtained at the expense of land forces. As a result of these actions, the Eisenhower administration was able to reduce taxes in 1954.

Did the international environment, aside from the termination of the war, permit these reduced defense outlays? Judged by Soviet military capabilities, which were improving, it would not seem so. Judged by the Eisenhower-Dulles rhetoric about the peril of the Soviets and the notion expressed in the Republican foreign policy platform of liberating captive peoples, there would seem no way of achieving large defense economies either. In the end, however, domestic considerations prevailed, and the economies were achieved. The resulting Eisenhower strategy was based on perceived Soviet intentions, not capabilities, and the liberation notion was never substituted for Truman's containment policy.

The New Look, in order to be credible, had to be sold to the NATO allies, who in any case had their own domestic reasons for wanting to be convinced that their defense pledges, involving as they did substantial ground forces, could be reduced. The United States, which in those days ran the alliance, sold the new strategy to NATO in two stages. In April 1953, the NATO council adopted Eisenhower's notion of the "long haul," meaning for NATO the stretch-out of their defense commitments. By the December 1954 NATO meeting, Congress had already blessed the New Look, and it was time for NATO to shift to a new strategy that placed major reliance on atomic weapons. The document that implemented this new strategy, and which was up for approval at the council meeting that month, was M.C. 48, which apparently had been inspired in large part by efforts of U.S. personnel, initially within SHAPE, and later within the NATO military committee staff.

Subsequently, there is no question that Sputnik accelerated U.S. efforts in missiles and related fields, probably far out of proportion to the satellite's military implications. Eisenhower took a more balanced view of the Soviet success than most, and the domestic economy was first in his mind. In order to pay the additional cost of new missile systems, defense outlays were reduced in other areas. Eisenhower also stuck with his 1956 decision for strategic sufficiency, rather than superiority over the Soviet Union, despite the "missile gap" and other forms of political pressure.

In the Berlin crisis of 1958–1959, Eisenhower's nuclear-heavy strategy, shaped largely by domestic budgetary considerations, was retained, even though the crisis caused some serious thinking about how to implement the strategy below the nuclear threshold. But no change was made in Eisenhower's strategy along the lines suggested by the logic of the limited-war school.

The point about the primacy of domestic budgetary deliberations should not be overdone, however. Strategic policy is, after all, directed in the main toward the external context in general and the perceived strategic threat in particular. Regardless of the importance of the domestic context in shaping strategic policy, the policy must still be adequate to meet the perceived threat. Normally there are several strategic policy options which would be adequate. A strategist concerned mainly with the external context would probably select a different option than a president who is concerned with both the domestic and external contexts.

Eisenhower's skepticism over basic strategy papers, such as the BNSP, is quite evident. In the meeting in his office in the summer of 1959 concerning the BNSP of that year, he openly questioned the validity of attempting to define strategy with the precision that was being attempted. McElroy's objection to changing the wording of the document was based on his desire to avoid other changes, as well as to avoid questions that might be raised by allies later. Obviously, if the wording of the document were important, such objections would not be seriously raised at presidential level. But from the evidence, it is apparent that basic strategy papers had little impact on defense budgets. There was no precise mix of forces or weaponry needed to carry out the Eisenhower strategy. The final force mix, which was expressed in terms of the defense budget, came about as a result of a political bargaining process dominated by the president. The outcome of this political bargaining, rather than a strategic policy paper, determined what strategic policy was to be pursued.

To generalize, this means not that strategic policy papers in themselves have no value, but rather that they are not the basis for the policy they articulate. A political bargaining process over the defense budget determined not only the budget itself, but what kind of strategic policy is to be pursued. When that political bargaining process is completed, a useful strategic policy paper can be written; earlier versions are drafts, however they may be labeled.

As Eisenhower indicated in his memoirs, he brought to the presidency what he called "logical guidelines for designing and employing a security establishment." These were what subsequently became the New Look, which Eisenhower defined as "first a reallocation of resources among the categories of forces, and second, the placing of greater emphasis than formerly on the deterrent and destructive power of improved nuclear weapons, better means of delivery, and effective air-defense units."

Eisenhower came to office with the strategic innovation he wanted to accomplish in mind and he achieved it by 1954. Before turning to Eisenhower's role in its retention, perhaps we should place the New Look itself in perspective.[1]

It was first of all a major strategic innovation. It was not a return to the Truman strategy of the period prior to the Korean War. Too much had changed for this to be possible. On the international scene the perceived adversary was growing increasingly stronger—militarily and economically. NSC-68, the last pre-Korean War look at strategy by the Truman administration, was both accepted and rejected by President Eisenhower. It was accepted in the sense that Eisenhower felt America should provide leadership to the non-Communist world. However, it was rejected in that military force was not to be based on "balanced" forces but on the strategic deterrent, at a time, moreover, when the adversary would soon be moving toward strategic parity.

Eisenhower perceived the nation's strength and security to be based on a fine balance between its economy and its military capabilities. There would be no more Koreas, which the adversary could initiate by proxy in any number of places around the world. Such actions would be deterred by serving notice that we would not become involved in a series of debilitating and expensive military engagements, but rather would respond selectively with nuclear power. Numerous instances have been cited in this study where Eisenhower made it clear that he had no intention of becoming involved in conventional wars, and he did not.

Eisenhower's role as the primary force in sustaining his strategic policy, which came under various forms of attack, is quite evident. His aggressiveness, confidence, and success in handling his adversaries, especially the service chiefs, come through quite clearly in the numerous meetings in his office. It is evident that the president dominated the defense budget process. Basically the technique he employed was to set a budget ceiling, usually called by another name, such as a target. He attempted to get the service chiefs to take what he called the broader outlook, that is, to accept his perceptions of the limitations of the U.S. economy. In part he succeeded in this: not, however, by getting them to accept their own budget ceilings, but rather in getting them to accept the overall budget ceiling.

It is interesting to note the way in which Eisenhower employed organizational procedures to retain the primacy of his role in defense matters. Specifically, he operated separate organizational channels for strategic policy and for the defense budget. For policy he dealt directly with the chairman of the Joint Chiefs of Staff, who in turn dealt with the service chiefs. For the budget, on the other hand, he dealt with the secretary of defense, whose budget channel then went directly to the services, the chairman not being involved routinely. What this meant was that the presidential level was the only one at which all aspects of strategic management came together; this was an enviable position for someone who wants to control both strategic policy and the defense budget.

The defense budget was the centerpiece of the overall Eisenhower budget and economic policy. The need for an executive consensus on it seems clear. A breakdown in executive consensus, especially if it led to public pressure on Congress for greater defense expenditures, would threaten the entire Eisenhower program. The evidence also gives considerable insight into the techniques employed by Eisenhower to gain executive consensus for his budget and his strategic policy. They included arguments based on the importance of a "sound" economy, insistence on a solid administration front in public and when testifying before Congress, and restricting information provided Congress, particularly about how certain policies were developed.

This is probably a good point to challenge against the conventional view that portrays Eisenhower as a rather passive president with Dulles calling the plays. It is frequently argued that Dulles was the prime mover or dominating figure in foreign policy during the Eisenhower administration. One of the support arguments sometimes used is Eisenhower's characterization of Dulles as the "greatest Secretary of State in history." In this regard an anecdote told by John S. D. Eisenhower is revealing: "With all the lumps that Dulles took in the press, probably only a very few people realize that he was essentially a very sensitive man. My Dad told me of this facet of his nature one evening when the two of us were walking through the lighted colonnade from the Mansion to the office. Dad observed that from time to time he was forced to make extravagant statements on the Secretary's abilities to sustain his morale. These statements, such as referring to Dulles as the 'greatest Secretary of State in history.' "[2]

Dulles had great rapport with Eisenhower. Yet, except for the early days of the administration, when his rapport was less than it was later, there is no evidence that his influence was great on matters of strategic policy. For one thing, he stayed out of the military infighting by choice. Also, he apparently did not want to weaken his power base with the president by challenging directly what he knew was a strategy to which Eisenhower was committed. Dulles never really asked the big questions about defense policies, which were, however, a large component of the administration's foreign policies. Evidence has been set forth that Dulles acquired misgivings about the New Look as the years went by, but he never really challenged the policy openly. He was influential with the president, but perhaps he felt not quite that influential.

Humphrey also enjoyed great rapport with Eisenhower, different from Dulles, but equally effective. There is no evidence that Humphrey got his own way in everything, but he was much less inhibited than Dulles about jumping into other areas of expertise. His understanding of strategic policy was not deep, but he understood the budgets. An economic conservative, he was quick to discern, and challenge, any threat to his budgetary objectives. Because of his ability in public debate, few of his colleagues wanted to take him on. One wonders how many challenges to Eisenhower's strategic policy he headed off, just by being at the National Security Council and other meetings on defense matters. One also suspects that Eisenhower was happy on many occasions to turn to him when the defense secretary was putting forth a strong Pentagon case for more resources. Robert Anderson, Humphrey's successor, was also highly regarded by Eisenhower. His economic outlook was similar to Humphrey's, and he was also tenacious and adroit in debate. By that time, however, Eisenhower did not need as much assistance in fending off the "requirements first" group, who had accommodated to the overall defense budget ceiling and were fighting with each other over the internal distribution.

Defense Secretaries Wilson and McElroy were both functionalists and neither had, relatively speaking, great rapport with the president. Their roles were to manage the Pentagon and to keep the lid on the defense budget. Neither secretary had a very sophisticated understanding of strategic policy, which is perhaps one reason Eisenhower chose them for the job. There is no evidence that Wilson had any great influence in developing the strategic rationale for the New Look or that McElroy ever got far afield from the defense budget or hardware debates. The two had different personalities, but they played the same role: defense secretaries who had relatively little influence on developing defense policy. Probably this outcome was inevitable, because of a number of things: Eisenhower's strong interest and prestige in strategic matters; the personalities and backgrounds of Wilson and McElroy; and, in McElroy's case, the relatively short period of time he was the defense secretary.

Several writers on the Eisenhower period have stressed the influence of the director of the Bureau of the Budget (of whom Eisenhower had four) in shaping U.S. strategy.[3] I have been unable to find any evidence that he did, in fact, do more than carry out presidential wishes, as far as the overall defense budget is concerned. The detailed programs in which the Bureau of the Budget exerted initiative on its own do not seem significant enough to warrant the implication that the director had an important role in shaping U.S. military posture. This is not to say that bureau guidance to the Defense Department on the defense budget was not significant. Except in technical matters, however, these directives did not really originate in the Bureau of the Budget. Insofar as I can determine, they carried out presidential directives precisely.

Although the Joint Chiefs are collectively responsible, by law, for providing military advice to the secretary of defense, the NSC, and the president, a strong chairman can easily insert himself between the service chiefs and higher political authority. This was particularly true of Admiral Radford, operating under ideal conditions because of his rapport with the president and Wilson. Perhaps the best example of this influence was his October 1953 talk in the NSC on the need for a decision on planning for early use of atomic weapons if defense budget economies were to be achieved. Radford was talking for himself, but to the NSC audience he appeared to be talking for the JCS. In addition to his rapport with his superiors, Radford had two specific advantages: his strategic and economic views were in harmony with the president, and he worked for a functionalist defense secretary who had little strategic understanding. It is true that Radford, as chairman, was at a disadvantage in having no real role in the budgetary process. He made up for that, however, by his influence with Wilson, so in fact he sometimes exercised an unofficial role in developing the defense budget. Radford's influence, although due to the circumstances of the time, could easily be repeated by different combinations of major actors and circumstances. The potential is there at any time.

The service chiefs during the Eisenhower period were able, aggressive, and in the main articulate; but except for the air force chiefs—and they were not entirely successful—their influence on strategic policy was not as great as they wished. From the president's point of view, however, they did not support his strategic policy to the extent that he wished. In attempting to bring the chiefs into a policy consensus, the president employed five techniques designed to influence the output of the national security process. These were careful selection and orientation of his top military advisers; conveying to them the role he expected them to play; insisting on loyalty or commitment to the administration's strategic policy; suppressing interservice disputes by stressing compromise and harmony; and reorganizing the Defense Department.

There is a fundamental contradiction involved here. The chiefs viewed themselves as military professionals, whose advice and goals were based on that professionalism. They were, in their opinion, apolitical. The president wanted to politicize the chiefs and to have them support the administration's strategic policy in their corporate role as the Joint Chiefs. He wanted them to rise above "national spirit and outlook." Eisenhower was asking too much; a service chief can never adopt such an approach (unless his service views coincide with the administration's) and still remain a service chief. Paul Hammond has put it well: "A service chief remains in effective control of his service only so long as he maintains its confidence; and nothing can cause the loss of that confidence faster than his abandonment of the role of service spokesman in the JCS."[4]

Eisenhower's search for consensus was understandable. Of course he could have obtained it with more liberal budgets to all the services, as did Kennedy later, but this was contrary to his conservative economic outlook.

Writers for the past dozen years or more have pointed out the piecemeal efforts of Congress when it comes to influencing strategic policy.[5] Limitations of staff, time, ability, information, and the pressures of other more immediate problems are among the reasons usually given to explain the inability of Congress to make any systematic review or contribution to U.S. strategic policy. This study has found essentially the same situation in the case of the Eisenhower strategic innovation in 1954 and in attempts to change it in 1959.

There is an exception in the movement toward the New Look in 1953. Specifically, the efforts of Robert Taft and certain other conservative Republicans did give a certain urgency to Eisenhower's initial efforts to reduce the defense budget, the outcome of which was, eventually, the New Look. This does not mean that Taft or any of his supporters systematically, or even on an ad hoc basis, examined the premises or rationale of the New Look. Their efforts were solely on the defense budget; but they, as contrasted to the congressional system as such, did push Eisenhower a little faster, but no further, than he wanted to go. Probably the circumstances were ideal for such an influence: a new president, who was going to innovate in any case, faced with a strong leader in his own party with whom he felt a strong requirement to cooperate.

In the 1959 congressional actions, however, the circumstances were in a sense reversed, and Congress was unable to make any change in the Eisenhower strategic policy. In this case Congress was controlled by the opposition party, many of whose leaders were critical of the administration's strategic policy and wanted to see changes. Some opposition leaders wanted increased budgetary outlays, and some wanted increased attention to limited-war forces. Eisenhower did not take the challenge lightly, but rather used many techniques to build consensus in the executive branch and to sell his program to Congress and the public.

In some ways congressmen seemed to have much going for them; there was a technologically unstable situation, and they were able to break down the appearance of consensus among the service chiefs. Congress did not shake public confidence in the president's strategic policy, however. The congressional efforts to influence strategic policy were unsystematic, superficial, and negligible. Although they were embarrassing to the administration and useful in the next presidential campaign, in the end Eisenhower retained his strategic innovation.

The classical critique of the Eisenhower NSC system was that of Senator Henry Jackson, published in 1960, in the form of a staff report by the Subcommittee on National Policy Machinery. The main conclusions of the report can be summarized as follows: the NSC should provide a forum where the president can meet with a small number of his department and agency heads, hear the policy alternatives, and provide guidance. The council had not worked that way, Jackson suggested, because of overcrowded agendas and overly elaborate procedures. What was needed was to deinstitutionalize the NSC process.[6] Jackson seems to have misled a decade of scholars with this rather simplistic critique of the Eisenhower NSC system, which was subsequently accepted as the conventional wisdom in the 1960s.

Jackson's critique was based on the assumption that the decision forum was the NSC; actually it was the Oval Office. There is, to be sure, the instance of October 13, 1953, when Radford's talk in the NSC about the need for authority to plan on using nuclear weapons at the outset of hostilities became the basis for the subsequent approval of the New Look. This talk came at the end of a long debate in which the conservative budgetary group, spearheaded by Humphrey, would not accept the cost of the force goals being proposed by the Defense Department. My own finding is that such important meetings were unusual in the NSC during the Eisenhower period, and intentionally so. Eisenhower did not want the NSC to have the same function Jackson thought it should have.

The evidence upon which I base that conclusion is of two types. First, there are the statements of those in a position to know. Goodpaster's statement in the Columbia Oral History Project is indirect, but the implication is clear when he told the interviewer that President Eisenhower had "many, many meetings in his office." John S. D. Eisenhower, Goodpaster's assistant, was more direct in his unpublished manuscript, when he said he thought his father regarded NSC meetings as a "debating society" and that the "real decisions were in the Oval Office with a small select group." McElroy's comments in the Columbia project were also direct when he told the interviewer that the decisions on anything important that he had anything to do with were made in the president's office.

The second type of evidence is the Oval Office meetings themselves. It is clearly evident that these discussions were unstructured in nature and directed toward solutions and decisions. The many instances where decisions were made in anticipation of council meetings, especially in the case of the budget, points up the relative importance of the two forums.

This is not to say that the NSC did not have an important function during the Eisenhower period, but rather that the function was somewhat different from that usually attributed to it. It was an ideal forum in which to achieve consensus, coordination, and to give an impetus to the implementation of decisions. Certainly the planning process, especially on lesser papers, promoted a healthy interaction among the agencies and departments concerned with strategic policy. It forced appropriate officials to confront major issues of national security and to evaluate the options. Whether the procedure was too elaborate or there was too much paperwork is not of much importance. Eisenhower had a use for the NSC, but it was not the use that Jackson criticized. The NSC that Jackson wanted was already at work in the Oval Office.

From this study I saw few instances where the key decisions on strategic policy were not made by the president in small informal meetings. This seemed to be his style of doing business. It is possible that his health, especially after the 1955 heart attack, worked against his participation in meaningful NSC or cabinet debates on major decisions, but that does not seem to be the key factor. It seems more related to Eisenhower's employment of his assistants in a way that maximized his influence on the outcome of strategic policy and defense budgets.

Eisenhower's military background gave him a confidence and aggressiveness in matters of strategic policy from the outset of his term as president. He brought to office definite views on the strategic policy he wanted the United States to follow. His political appointees to the key secretarial positions at the State, Defense, and Treasury departments were such that they would be supportive of his objectives in strategic matters. The military chiefs were another matter, and he was never able to gain fully their cooperation, except for the chairman and usually the air force chief, whose strategic views were harmonious with his own.

Eisenhower's argument for the New Look was not sophisticated, but he believed it and insisted that others believe it. His feeling was that the economy was the pillar of U.S. strength and security, and unbalanced budgets threatened that pillar. When confronted with classical arguments of the need for limited-war forces, his rejoinder was simple. If the United States had enough power to fight a big war, it also had enough power for a little one.

From my research it is clear that in matters of strategic policy formulation and implementation, Eisenhower's confidence, background, great skill in handling subordinates, generally good relations with Congress, and, most important, his wide public support made him exceedingly strong.[7] There is no question as his term in office progressed he encountered an increasingly rebellious Pentagon and restive Congress in defense matters. Nevertheless, through bureaucratic skill, and employing his wide public appeal, he was able to sustain his strategic innovation against those who wanted to change it.

In sum, contrary to the conventional picture of Eisenhower as a passive president, he emerges as a skilled practitioner of closed politics who dominated and frequently manipulated a very powerful set of political and military appointees. In the making and management of strategic policy he was a strong, active, and effective president.

# *Notes*

PREFACE

1. See, for example, Marquis Childs, *Eisenhower: Captive Hero* (New York: Harcourt Brace, 1958); James D. Barber, *The Presidential Character* (New York: Prentice Hall, 1972); Norman A. Graebner, "Eisenhower's Popular Leadership," in *Eisenhower as President*, ed. Dean Albertson (New York: Hill and Wang, 1963); Emmet John Hughes, *The Living Presidency* (New York: Coward, McCann, and Geohegan, 1972); Richard E. Neustadt, *Presidential Power* (New York: John Wiley and Sons, 1960); George E. Reedy, *The Twilight of the Presidency* (New York: World, 1970); Richard H. Rovere, *The Eisenhower Years* (New York: Farrar, Straus, and Cudahy, 1956); and Arthur M. Schlesinger, Jr., *The Imperial Presidency* (Boston: Houghton Mifflin, 1973).

2. Nixon, *Six Crises* (New York: Pyramid Books, 1968), p. 172; Larson, *Eisenhower: The President Nobody Knew* (New York: Scribner's, 1968), p. 198; Kempton, *Esquire* (September 1967), p. 108.

CHAPTER ONE

1. There is a tendency to stereotype Robert Taft as an isolationist. Although he obviously was not as much of an internationalist as Eisenhower, his outlook was too complex to be described by any simple label. For a perceptive treatment of this, see Peter Lyon, *Eisenhower: Portrait of the Hero* (Boston: Little, Brown, 1974), pp. 391, 392.

2. Eisenhower's conservative economic views were genuine. To Eisenhower the U.S. economy was like the source of a mother's milk—tender and soft and not to be abused. His son, John S. D. Eisenhower, in correspondence

with me in 1974, indicated that his father's economic views began to form during his first tour of duty on the Army General Staff from 1927 to 1935. For an interesting account of how these views were carefully nurtured during the period 1948 to 1952 by a number of Republicans who wanted Ike to run for president, see Lyon, *Eisenhower*, pp. 381–439. Lyon (p. 421) cites an Eisenhower letter written while he was supreme commander in early 1951 to Edward J. Bermingham, a wealthy retired investment banker, which is illustrative of his keen interest in the U.S. economy: "the only way we can achieve military success either in preventing war or in winning a war is through preserving the integrity of our economy and our financial structure."

3. Robert J. Donovan, *Eisenhower: The Inside Story* (New York: Harper, 1956), pp. 108–11. There are numerous other accounts of this incident, all of which are substantially the same. Eisenhower tells it himself in *The White House Years*, vol. 1, *Mandate for Change* (New York: Doubleday, 1963), pp. 129–31.

4. Leonard Lurie, *The King Makers* (New York: Coward, McCann, and Geohagen, 1971), p. 233; Donovan, *Inside Story*, p. 103; Eisenhower, *Mandate for Change*, p. 64.

5. Eisenhower, *Mandate for Change*, p. 192.

6. Ibid., p. 95; *New York Times*, December 15, 1952, p. 6; Eisenhower, *Mandate for Change*, p. 181.

7. In the words of the irrepressible secretary of the treasury, George M. Humphrey, at a cabinet meeting on May 1, 1953: "To get real tax reduction you have to get Korea out of the way. And after that you have to go on and do something more—figure out a completely new military posture. . . . We have to cut one-third out of the budget, and you can't do that just by eliminating waste. This means, wherever necessary, using a meat ax." Quoted in Emmet John Hughes, *The Ordeal of Power* (New York: Atheneum, 1963), p. 72.

8. U.S., Congress, House, Committee on Appropriations, Defense Appropriations Subcommittee (hereafter HSAC), *Department of Air Force Appropriations Hearings FY 1954*, 83d Cong., 1st sess., 1953, pp. 959, 960.

9. Paul Y. Hammond, "NSC-68," in Warner R. Schilling, Paul Y. Hammond, and Glenn H. Snyder, *Strategy, Politics, and Defense Budgets* (New York: Columbia University Press, 1962), pp. 267–378. The document was declassified in February 1975. It is reproduced in the *Naval War College Review*, May-June 1975.

10. Donovan, *Inside Story*, pp. 17–18, and Hughes, *Ordeal*, pp. 40–52; Samuel P. Huntington, *The Common Defense* (New York: Columbia University Press, 1961), pp. 197, 198.

11. U.S., National Archives, *Public Papers of the Presidents of the United States*, 1953 (Washington, D.C.: Government Printing Office, 1960), p. 242; hereafter cited as *Public Papers*.

12. Louis L. Gerson, *John Foster Dulles* (New York: Cooper Square, 1967), p. 133.

13. Eisenhower, *Mandate for Change*, pp. 445–47.

14. As compared to the United States' 1,000. *New York Times*, December 10, 1953, p. 9.

15. John Foster Dulles, "Where Are We?" (Address to American Association for the United Nations, New York, December 29, 1950).

16. John Foster Dulles Papers (Princeton University Library), 10:483, letter dated April 15, 1952; hereafter cited as JFD Coll. According to Eisen-

hower, this letter "began between us an active association and exchange of views which was to grow in intimacy and breadth during the next seven years"; Eisenhower, *Mandate for Change*, p. 23. There is a possible inconsistency here between Eisenhower's skepticism concerning Dulles's "retaliation" notion and his own reliance on deterrence, which was a strategic concept he considered basic and valid at the time he became president. Perhaps this can be explained by Eisenhower's role change from supreme allied commander, Europe, to president of the United States.

17. John Foster Dulles, "A Policy of Boldness," *Life* (May 19, 1952), pp. 146–60.

18. JFD Coll., 10:483, letter dated May 20, 1952. The platform is reproduced in K. H. Porter and D. B. Johnson, comps., *National Party Platforms, 1840–1960* (Urbana: University of Illinois Press, 1961), pp. 496–505.

19. Multilateral: Inter-American Treaty of Reciprocal Assistance (Rio Pact 1947); North Atlantic Treaty (1949); and Australia, New Zealand, United States (1951). Bilateral: with the Philippines (1951). Executive Agreements: with Denmark concerning the defense of Greenland (1951); and Iceland (1951).

20. Robert E. Osgood, *NATO: The Entangling Alliance* (Chicago: University of Chicago Press, 1962), p. 49.

21. For example, see the statement by President Harry S. Truman in *U.S. Department of State Bulletin* 22 (July 3, 1950): 5.

22. *New York Times*, September 10, 1950, p. 1.

23. Osgood, *NATO*, p. 75.

24. *National Security Act of 1947* as amended. Statutory members were the president, vice president, secretaries of state and defense, and the director of the Office of Civil and Defense Mobilization (subsequently called the Office of Emergency Preparedness). Statutory advisers were the chairman of the Joint Chiefs of Staff and director of the CIA.

25. Robert Cutler, *No Time for Rest* (Boston: Little, Brown, 1965), pp. 296–98.

26. Ibid., pp. 298, 299. Interview with S. Everett Gleason, deputy executive secretary to NSC, 1950–1959, April 12, 1972.

27. Keith C. Clark and Laurence J. Legere, eds., *The President and the Management of National Security* (New York: Praeger, 1969), p. 218.

28. Ibid., p. 60; John S. D. Eisenhower, *Strictly Personal* (New York: Doubleday, 1974), pp. 204–6; Andrew J. Goodpaster, transcript, "Columbia Oral History Project." Quote from John S. D. Eisenhower, unpublished manuscript (1972); in JSDE's private papers, Phoenixville, Pa.

29. Henry M. Jackson, ed., *The National Security Council: Jackson Subcommittee Papers on Policy-Making at the Presidential Level* (New York: Praeger, 1965), esp. pp. 38–39; Dwight D. Eisenhower, "The Central Role of the President in the Conduct of Security Affairs," in *Issues of National Security in the 1970's*, ed. Amos A. Jordan, Jr. (New York: Praeger, 1967), p. 214.

30. For an early example, see "Thoughts on Soviet Foreign Policy and What to Do about It," in *Life* (June 3 and 10, 1946).

31. Sherman Adams, transcript, "Dulles Oral History Project," Princeton University Library (hereafter referred to as DOH); Eisenhower, *The White House Years*, vol. 2, *Waging Peace* (New York, Doubleday, 1965), pp. 367–68.

32. See, for example, discussion on this question in transcripts of Dillon

Anderson and Robert R. Bowie in DOH. See also Lyon, *Eisenhower*, pp. 510, 511.

33. Roderic L. O'Connor, transcript, DOH.

34. Adams, transcript, DOH; Bowie, transcript, DOH.

35. Eisenhower, *Mandate for Change*, p. 87. Clay, along with Herbert Brownell, was an adviser to Eisenhower on the selection of his cabinet.

36. Hughes, *Ordeal*, pp. 72, 73; Maxwell D. Taylor, *Swords and Plowshares* (New York: Norton, 1972), p. 170.

37. Eisenhower, *Mandate for Change*, p. 87; Robert Sprague, transcript, DOH.

38. Sherman Adams, *Firsthand Report* (New York: Harper, 1961), p. 56.

39. Carter Burgess, transcript, "Columbia Oral History Project," and transcripts of Sherman Adams, Arthur Radford, and Thomas Gates in DOH.

40. Eisenhower, *Mandate for Change*, pp. 96, 455 n.

41. Ibid., passim. John S. D. Eisenhower, unpublished manuscript (1972); Arthur Radford, transcript, DOH; Maxwell D. Taylor, *The Uncertain Trumpet* (New York: Harper, 1959), passim.

42. Apolitical was a word with which then Army Chief of Staff William Westmoreland described his role in a meeting with me in August 1971.

43. Matthew B. Ridgway, *Soldier* (New York: Harper, 1956), passim.

44. A frequent explanation of the early date is, however, Vandenberg's terminal illness, from which he died nine months after retirement.

45. Robert B. Carney, "Principles of Sea Power," *U.S. Naval Institute Proceedings* 81 (September 1955): 985.

46. Twining had already been sworn in.

47. The categories were 1) nuclear retaliatory; 2) land forces and tactical air forces stationed overseas; 3) naval and marine forces in the Atlantic and Pacific charged with keeping the sea lanes open; 4) continental air defense units; and 5) strategic reserve forces in the U.S. Eisenhower, *Mandate for Change*, p. 451.

48. Arthur Radford, transcript, DOH.

49. Snyder, *New Look*, pp. 414, 424.

50. This meeting is an outstanding exception to the previous discussion on Eisenhower's use of the NSC. It is described by Joseph and Stewart Alsop in the *New York Herald Tribune*, February 22, 1954. Also in "Defense and Strategy," *Fortune* (December 1953), pp. 77, 78, 82, 84.

51. This paper is now available as part of the *Pentagon Papers*, Gravel edition (Boston: Beacon Press, 1971), 1:412–29.

52. HSAC, *Department of Defense Appropriations Hearings, FY 1957*, 84th Cong., 2d sess., p. 610.

53. *New York Times*, November 11, 1953, p. 17.

54. *Vital Speeches of the Day* 20 (January 1, 1954): 171–73.

55. Contained in *Public Papers*, 1954, starting at pp. 6, 79, and 215 respectively.

56. The text of the speech discussed here is in State Department press release 8 of 1954. Official distribution of this item was 100,000. The last sentence quoted was penned onto page 10 of a draft of the speech which had been sent to the president for comment, in what appears to be Eisenhower's handwriting, JFD Coll. Eisenhower himself addressed the matter of commenting on Dulles's speeches in *Waging Peace*, p. 365. "He [Dulles] would never deliver an important speech or statement until after I had read, edited, and approved it; he guarded constantly against the possibility that any misunder-

standing could arise between us." Halle (*Cold War as History*, p. 281) is wrong when he says Dulles showed the speech only to a State Department lawyer in advance of its delivery.

57. Radford, transcript, DOH; George Humphrey, transcript, DOH.

58. Nathan Twining, transcript, DOH; Robert Bowie, transcript, DOH. In addition to the American public, Dulles was also talking to the U.S. allies, especially NATO, both to reassure them of a firm U.S. commitment and to encourage them to adopt the proposed European Defense Community, then under consideration.

59. Some of the early critics were Chester Bowles, writing in the *New York Times Magazine* of February 28, and Adlai Stevenson, titular head of the Democratic party, speaking in Miami on March 6. Dulles felt almost immediately the need to clarify his speech, which he attempted to do in the next issue of *Foreign Affairs*. In the article he seemed more flexible than in the council speech. The change in rhetoric had no impact on the New Look as a strategic policy, however, or on the defense budget, which provided the resources to carry out the strategic policy.

It is probably worth noting that the phenomenon of McCarthyism which had plagued the United States since the early 1950s reached its peak during the army-McCarthy hearings in the spring of 1954 at the same time as congressional consideration of the fiscal year 1955 budget. I will leave to other writers the question of Eisenhower's handling of McCarthy and the effect of McCarthy's efforts on the morale of government employees and others; the question of interest to me is whether McCarthy's activities had an important effect on strategic policy debates. No doubt in a broad sense they did by exacerbating cold war tensions, at least within the American polity, thus, for example, escalating Eisenhower's rhetoric about communism in the 1952 election and afterwards. I can find no specific evidence, however, that in any major way they directly influenced Eisenhower's strategic concepts or the amount of budgetary resources he was willing to commit to national security. Some of the better discussions of the McCarthy problem that Eisenhower had to contend with and judgments on his effectiveness in the handling of McCarthy are contained in Lyon, *Eisenhower;* Herbert S. Parmet, *Eisenhower and the American Crusades* (New York: Macmillan, 1972); and Lately Thomas, *When Even Angels Wept* (New York: William Morrow, 1973).

60. Eisenhower, *Mandate for Change*, pp. 192, 193.

61. Adams, *Firsthand Report*, p. 9.

62. Hughes, *Ordeal*, p. 126; Eisenhower, *Mandate for Change*, p. 298.

63. Hughes, *Ordeal*, p. 128. Another discussion of Eisenhower as a Whig is in Schlesinger, *Imperial Presidency*, pp. 152, 153.

64. Continental air defense was another problem inherited from the Truman administration. As early as 1950 and 1951 respectively, Army Antiaircraft and Air Force Air Defense commands were created in recognition of a growing Soviet strategic bombardment threat. A series of studies—some begun in the Truman period and some done early in the Eisenhower period—had recognized the problem and proposed greater emphasis on continental defense. With the explosion of the Soviet hydrogen bomb in August 1953 the matter was given increased emphasis and merged with New Look policy decisions. Eisenhower's decisions in October 1953 included increased recognition of continental air defense as a major defense need and provisions for increased budgetary support. This was a major defense decision. In 1954 a Continental Air Defense Command involving all military services was established, and

in 1957 the North American Air Defense Command was established which provided for Canadian and American participation.

65. HSAC, *Department of Defense Appropriations Hearings, FY 1955*, 83d Cong., 2d sess., 1954, p. 67.

66. HSAC, *Department of Army Appropriations Hearings, FY 1955*, 83d Cong., 2d sess., 1954, p. 3.

67. HSAC, *Department of Navy Appropriations Hearings, FY 1955*, 83d Cong., 2d sess., 1954, p. 66.

68. HSAC, *Department of Air Force Appropriations Hearings, FY 1955*, 83d Cong., 2d sess., 1954, pp. 51–52.

69. U.S., Congress, House, *Congressional Record* (hereafter cited as C.R.), 83d Cong., 2d sess., C, pt 4: 5671.

70. Ibid., pp. 5684–85.

71. Ibid., pt. 5: 5748–49.

72. U.S., Congress, Senate, Committee on Appropriations (hereafter cited as SSAC). Defense Appropriations Subcommittee, *Department of Defense Appropriations Hearings, FY 1955*, 83d Cong., 2d sess., 1954, pp. 43–44.

73. Ibid., p. 83.

74. Ridgway, *Soldier*, p. 272. This book also contains a statement by Ridgway which makes one wonder if he had sufficient Washington experience for the job he held. "The real situation then dawned on me. This military budget was not based so much on military requirements or on what the economy of the country could stand, as on political considerations."

75. U.S., Congress, Senate, Committee on Foreign Relations, *Foreign Policy and Its Relation to Military Programs, Hearings*, 83d Cong., 2d sess., 1954, p. 20.

76. Ibid., p. 43.

77. C.R., 83d Cong., 2d sess., C, pt. 6: 8328, 8432, 8433. At that time the situation in Indochina was still in everyone's mind. In late March 1954 the French asked for massive U.S. air intervention during the siege of Dien Bien Phu. The British government was opposed to such intervention, and those U.S. congressmen who became involved in discussions on this matter opposed any intervention without the support of allies. As for the use of U.S. ground troops, Ridgway felt it unwise, considering what troops were available, and the president agreed with him. In the end, the United States did not intervene at that time, and the Geneva Accords soon came along.

78. Ibid., p. 8342.

79. This is not surprising. As Huntington pointed out in 1961 (*Common Defense*, p. 223): "The budget is still a principal means of civilian control of the military, but it is a weapon wielded by executive agencies, not congressional ones."

CHAPTER TWO

1. Angus Campbell et al., *The American Voter* (New York: John Wiley, 1960), pp. 44–59.

2. Huntington, *Common Defense*, pp. 259–64.

3. As it turned out, the 83d Congress was the only Republican Congress during the Eisenhower presidency. The following table shows the margins in each case.

HOUSE

| Election | 1952 | 1954 | 1956 | 1958 |
|---|---|---|---|---|
| Democrats | 213 | 232 | 234 | 282 |
| Republicans | 221 | 203 | 201 | 154 |
| Other | 1 | | | |

SENATE

| Election | 1952 | 1954 | 1956 | 1958 |
|---|---|---|---|---|
| Democrats | 47 | 48 | 49 | 64 |
| Republicans | 48 | 47 | 47 | 34 |
| Other | 1 | 1 | | |

4. Arnold L. Horelick and Myron Rush, *Strategic Power and Soviet Foreign Policy* (Chicago: University of Chicago Press, 1966), p. 27.

5. Allen Dulles, *The Craft of Intelligence* (New York: Harper and Row, 1963), p. 149.

6. Horelick and Rush, *Strategic Power*, p. 30.

7. Ibid., p. 31.

8. Osgood, *NATO*, p. 119; quote from U.S., Library of Congress, *U.S. Policy on the Use of Nuclear Weapons, 1945–75* (Washington, D.C.: Congressional Research Service, 1975), p. 51.

9. Interview with Maxwell Taylor, Washington, D.C., August 1972.

10. Memorandum of Conference with the President (hereafter cited as MCP), February 24, 1955. Note entries such as these, of which there are many, refer to meetings with the president on which notes were taken by his staff. These notes which were converted into documents are not classified but are as of October 1976 still considered privileged. I was allowed to examine the documents and to take notes. Where quotations are shown, they are direct quotes of the speaker indicated. Sometimes they were written as a Memorandum for Record.

11. Radford, transcript, DOH.

12. Taylor, *Uncertain Trumpet*, recounts the frustrations he encountered in trying to put across his strategic ideas.

13. Letter from Edward L. Beach to Kinnard, July 18, 1974.

14. Ken Jones and Hubert Kelley, Jr., *Admiral Arleigh (31-Knot) Burke* (Philadelphia: Chilton, 1962), pp. 166–277, 172.

15. Interview with Edward L. Beach, August 17, 1972.

16. The best guide to this literature is a bibliography by Morton H. Halperin, *Limited War in the Nuclear Age* (New York: John Wiley, 1963).

17. Brodie, "Unlimited Weapons and Limited War," *Reporter* 11 (November 18, 1954): 16–21; Kaufmann, ed., *Military Policy and National Security* (Princeton, N.J.: Princeton University Press, 1956), pp. 12–38.

18. Blackett, *Atomic Energy and East-West Relations* (Cambridge: Cambridge University Press, 1956), p. 100; Buzzard et al., *On Limiting Nuclear War* (London: Royal Institute of International Affairs, 1956); Blackett, "Nuclear Weapons and Defense," *International Affairs* 34 (October 1958).

19. Henry A. Kissinger, *Nuclear Weapons and Foreign Policy* (New York: Harper, 1957). By 1960 Kissinger had second thoughts and felt that although tactical nuclear weapons had a place in the arsenal, they could not take the

place of conventional forces; Kissinger, *The Necessity for Choice* (New York: Harper, 1960).

20. Kaufmann, "The Crisis in Military Affairs," *World Politics* 10 (July 1958):579–603.

21. Osgood, *Limited War: The Challenge to American Strategy* (Chicago: University of Chicago Press, 1957).

22. Michael Howard, "The Classical Strategists," in *National Security and American Society*, ed. Frank N. Traeger and Philip S. Kromenberg (Manhattan: University Press of Kansas, 1973), p. 290.

23. Wohlstetter, "The Delicate Balance of Terror," *Foreign Affairs* 37 (January 1959):211–34.

24. Morgenstern, *The Question of National Defense* (New York: Random House, 1959), p. 75; Brodie, *Strategy in the Missile Age* (Princeton, N.J.: Princeton University Press, 1959), p. 330.

25. For a trenchant critique of these writings and their failure to explore major foreign policy alternatives, see Morris Janowitz, "Toward a Redefinition of Military Strategy in International Relations," *World Politics* (July 1974): 487, 488.

26. Annual Presidential Budget Message, January 16, 1956, in *Public Papers*, 1956, pp. 75–92.

27. Unpublished manuscript, "Office of the Secretary of the Army, 1955–1960," filed in Office of the Chief of Military History, United States Army, Washington, D.C.

28. Testimony of Admiral Arleigh Burke before the Senate Committee on Armed Services, June 18, 1956. Excerpts in Eugene M. Emme, ed., *The Impact of Air Power* (New York: Van Nostrand, 1959), p. 682. U.S., Congress, House, *United States Defense Policies since World War II*, H. Doc. 100, 85th Cong., 1st sess., 1957.

29. For example, see Joseph Alsop's article in the *Washington Post*, August 21, 1955, in which he discussed a Soviet missile of 1,500-mile range.

30. MCP, February 10, 1956.

31. Memorandum for Chairman, Joint Chiefs of Staff, from Office of the President, February 17, 1956.

32. Edward A. Kolodziej, *The Uncommon Defense and Congress, 1945–1963* (Columbus: Ohio State University Press, 1966), p. 236; MCP, March 13, 1956.

33. MCP, March 30, 1956.

34. MCP, April 3, 1956.

35. MCP, April 5, 1956.

36. MCP, April 18, 1956.

37. Ridgway, "My Battles in War and Peace: Conflict in the Pentagon," *Saturday Evening Post* (January 21, 1956); and Ridgway, *Soldier*.

38. MCP, May 14, 1956.

39. MCP, March 30, 1956, May 14, 1956.

40. MCP, May 24, 1956; Taylor describes the background for this confrontation in *Uncertain Trumpet*, pp. 36–46.

41. Thomas N. Schroth, ed., *Congress and the Nation, 1945–1964* (Washington: Congressional Quarterly Service, 1965), p. 294.

42. Taylor, *Uncertain Trumpet*, pp. 39 ff.

43. MCP, July 31, 1956.

44. MCP, October 11, 1956.

45. Memorandum from Secretary of the Navy to Secretary of Defense, cited

in U.S., Congress, House, Armed Services Committee on Military Posture, *Hearings*, 89th Cong., 2d sess., 1966, pp. 80–84.

46. Excerpts from the Symington Hearings report are in Emme, *Impact of Air Power*, pp. 697–705.

47. Robert F. Futrell, *Ideas, Concepts, Doctrine: A History of Basic Thinking in the United States Air Force* (Montgomery, Ala.: Air University, 1971), 1:464, 468.

48. Quarles, "The Uses of Modern Arms," *Flying* (February 1957), pp. 25–26.

49. MCP, November 8, 1956.

50. MCP, December 7, 1956-.

51. MCP, December 19, 1956. No doubt these comments of Eisenhower seem elliptical—as indeed they were.

52. MCP, December 21, 1956.

53. Memorandum for Record, January 12, 1957.

54. The text of Humphrey's most famous press conference is contained in Nathaniel R. Howard, ed., *The Basic Papers of George M. Humphrey* (Cleveland: Western Reserve Historical Society, 1965), pp. 236–52. Eisenhower, *Waging Peace*, p. 129.

55. MCP, January 12, 1957.


CHAPTER THREE

1. "Precisely at the moment of his re-election, history caught up with him in giant steps: Hungary and Suez. . . . Others followed after"; Neustadt, *Presidential Power*, p. 167.

2. Eisenhower tells the recession story in *Waging Peace*, pp. 305 ff. Good contemporary accounts are Charles J. V. Murphy, "The White House and the Recession," *Fortune* (May 1958), pp. 106–9 and 242–52, and Ivan Hinderaker, "The Eisenhower Administration: The Last Years," in *American Government Annual, 1959–1960*, ed. Jack W. Peltason (New York: Holt-Dryden, 1959), pp. 69–91. A more recent view in a broader perspective is in James L. Sundquist, *Politics and Policy* (Washington: Brookings, 1968).

3. Hans J. Morgenthau, *Dilemmas of Politics* (Chicago: University of Chicago Press, 1958), p. 337.

4. Huntington, *Common Defense*, p. 255.

5. Horelick and Rush, *Strategic Power*, pp. 50–52.

6. For a good treatment of this controversy, see Edgar M. Bottome, *The Missile Gap* (Rutherford, N.J.: Fairleigh Dickinson Press, 1971); Eisenhower *Waging Peace*, pp. 389, 390.

7. A Khrushchev press conference and speech directed toward NATO in the spring of 1959 are cited in Horelick and Rush, *Strategic Power*, p. 55 n.; Eisenhower, *Waging Peace*, pp. 348, 349.

8. Eisenhower, *Waging Peace*, pp. 290, 291. As for the political aspects of the Lebanon affair, there are numerous accounts that differ from Eisenhower's. For a perceptive treatment, see Lyon, *Eisenhower*, pp. 771–76.

9. Although an impression was left that in some cases the use of tactical nuclear weapons "might not lead to total war, the United States and her allies were not basing their strategy on this expectation in the NATO area but rather on the probability that any conventional aggression in Europe

would lead to nuclear war and any nuclear war would lead to unlimited nuclear war." Osgood, *NATO*, pp. 160, 162.

10. MCP, September 12, 1960; Memorandum for Record, December 23, 1957.

11. James Shepley, "How Dulles Averted War," *Life* (January 16, 1956). To be fair, the exact wording was Shepley's, not Dulles's, but the image fits. Robert Bowie believed Dulles used this technique although he did not specifically relate it to this instance. Bowie, transcript, DOH. Herter, transcript, DOH.

12. Taylor, transcript, DOH; Burke, transcript, DOH.

13. John S. D. Eisenhower, unpublished manuscript (1972).

14. Ibid. Humphrey, transcript, DOH.

15. John S. D. Eisenhower, unpublished manuscript (1972); Eisenhower, *Waging Peace*, pp. 7 n., 359, 591.

16. One of his more famous analogies was the one between people and dogs. He himself favored bird dogs over kennel dogs, who "simply sit on their fannies and yell."

17. McElroy, transcript, "Columbia Oral History Project."

18. Carl W. Borklund, *Men of the Pentagon* (New York: Praeger, 1966), p. 180.

19. Taylor, *Uncertain Trumpet*, p. 110; John S. D. Eisenhower, unpublished manuscript (1972); Twining, *Neither Liberty nor Safety* (New York: Holt, Rinehart, 1966), p. 148.

20. MCP, July 10, 1957.

21. Eisenhower, *Waging Peace*, pp. 210–12; MCP, October 9 and 11, 1957.

22. MCP, October 30, 1957.

23. A strongly partisan view of this issue is contained in "Office of the Secretary of the Army" (unpublished manuscript, Office of Military History, Washington, D.C.), pp. 84–86.

24. Burke, "Problems Confronting the Navy Today" (Speech to the Naval War College, September 9, 1957); Burke, "Remarks at Naval Commandants Conference," December 2, 1957; both contained in Operational Archives, Naval History Division, Washington, D.C.

25. Burke, "Remarks at Naval Commandants Conference," pp. 5–6.

26. Ibid., p. 7.

27. Robert F. Futrell, *Air Force Thinking* (Montgomery, Ala.: Air University, 1971), p. 472.

28. See Eisenhower, *Waging Peace*, pp. 219–33, for his full perspective on the Gaither report. A good treatment of the case by a political scientist who stresses the zealousness of certain members of the group in trying to sell their case to Eisenhower and others is Morton H. Halperin. "The Gaither Committee and the Policy Process," *World Politics* 13 (April 1961): 360–84.

29. MCP, October 29 and November 4, 1957.

30. Eisenhower, *Waging Peace*, p. 221.

31. Ibid.

32. Excerpts of speech are in Emme, *Impact of Air Power*, pp. 711–18.

33. Memorandum for Record, November 4, 1957.

34. MCP, November 11, 1957.

35. MCP, November 15, 1957.

36. MCP, November 22, 1957.

37. Memorandum for Record, December 2, 1957.

38. *Public Papers*, 1958, pp. 4, 17–24.

39. Memorandum for Record, December 23, 1957.

40. In the Dulles Oral History, these include Gerard Smith (Dulles's policy planning chief after Bowie), Arleigh Burke, Neil McElroy, and Thomas Gates. Notes drafted by the State Department staff for Dulles's use in talking to the service chiefs at Quantico in June 1957 give some evidence of this; JFD Coll., 10:482.

41. At the meeting, in addition to Dulles and McElroy, there were Donald Quarles, Wilber Brucker, Thomas Gates, Thomas White, James Douglas, Robert Sprague, Nathan Twining, Maxwell Taylor, Randolph Pate, Arleigh Burke, Gerard Smith, Lewis Strauss, Robert Cutler, and Andrew Goodpaster. Memorandum for Record, April 9, 1958.

42. Taylor, *Uncertain Trumpet*, pp. 59–65; Gerard Smith, transcript, DOH.

43. MCP, June 24, 1958.

44. MCP, November 4, 1957.

In his first year in office Eisenhower had, within his own authority, signed Reorganization Plan Six which, after some opposition in Congress, became effective on June 30, 1953. Two parts of the plan are worth noting here: 1) Within the Defense Department, the number of assistant secretaries was increased threefold at the expense of separate boards and agencies such as the Munitions Board and the Research and Development Board. This change provided a clearer channel between the secretary of defense and his department as well as a potential for better central control. The expectation was that he could exercise greater control of the department's budgetary and administrative activities. 2) The reorganization improved the cohesiveness of the Joint Staff and strengthened the position of the chairman. Prior to the reorganization, appointments to the staff were not cleared by the chairman. It is easy to imagine the difficulties that this situation caused the chairman, sitting in the same building with highly integrated, very powerful service staffs who would fill "their" vacancies on his staff. Eisenhower, in *Mandate for Change*, stated as his objective to divorce "the thinking and the outlook of the members of the Joint Staff from those of the parent services and to center their entire effort on national planning for the over-all common defense."

45. Eisenhower, *Waging Peace*, pp. 244, 245; Memorandum for Record, January 30, 1958.

46. Eisenhower, *Waging Peace*, p. 245; Memorandum for Record, January 25, 1958.

47. Eisenhower, *Waging Peace*, pp. 244–53.

48. U.S., Congress, House, *Recommendations Relative to Our Entire Defense Establishment*, H. Doc. 366, 85th Cong., 2d sess., 1958.

49. Eisenhower, *Waging Peace*, p. 250; Memorandum for Record, April 9, 1958.

50. Jones and Kelley, *Arleigh Burke*, p. 191; MCP, June 23, 1958.

51. U.S., Congress, *Department of Defense Reorganization Act of 1958*, S. 3649 and H.R. 11958, 85th Cong., 2d sess., 1958.

52. MCP, April 21, 1958.

53. Eisenhower, *Waging Peace*, p. 252. Public Law 85-599, 85th Cong., 2d sess. Signed by the president on August 6, 1958.

54. Eisenhower, *Waging Peace*, pp. 385, 386.

55. Memorandum for Record, March 7, 1958. As Schlesinger points out in *The Imperial Presidency*, pp. 156–59, Eisenhower in 1955 had added an al-

most unlimited category of information which was denied to Congress at the presidential will, i.e., material generated by the internal deliberative processes of government. This was a claim of executive privilege going far beyond the president's immediate aides to the executive branch as a whole.

56. Eisenhower, *Waging Peace*, p. 389; MCP, August 29 and October 7, 1958. Symington sets forth his own version of the "missile gap" in an article, "Where the Missile Gap Went," *Reporter* 26 (February 15, 1962).

57. MCP, November 28, 1958.

58. Memorandum for Record, December 3, 1958.

59. Taylor, *Uncertain Trumpet*, p. 72.

60. *Public Papers*, 1959, p. 8; Eisenhower, *Waging Peace*, p. 387.

61. The interested senators were Lyndon B. Johnson, Richard B. Russell, Stuart Symington, Henry M. Jackson, John Stennis, and Carl Hayden. The representatives were George Mahon, Robert Sikes, Daniel Flood, Gerald Ford, Melvin Laird, Carl Vinson, and Paul Kilday.

62. HSAC, *Defense Appropriations, FY 1960*, 86th Cong., 1st sess., 1959, pp. 74, 121.

63. Ibid., pp. 78, 132.

64. Ibid., p. 145.

65. Ibid., p. 433.

66. Ibid., p. 582.

67. Ibid., p. 881.

68. MCP, February 9, 1959.

69. HSAC, *Defense Appropriations, FY 1960*, pp. 77–78, 206.

70. Ibid., pp. 329–31.

71. Ibid., pp. 505–9, 536–38. The Polaris submarine he wanted would be an increase in the total program from nine to ten.

72. Ibid., pp. 824–27.

73. Speech reprinted in ibid., pp. 97–101; see pp. 96–104.

74. Ibid., pp. 344–45, 320.

75. Ibid., pp. 548, 549, 566, 567.

76. Ibid., pp. 804, 874.

77. SSAC, *Defense Appropriations, FY 1960*, 86th Cong., 1st sess., 1959, pp. 4, 16.

78. Ibid., pp. 20–22.

79. The army's Nike-Hercules was designed to provide protection from enemy aircraft in the vicinity of a potential target. The air force's Bomarc, of greater range, was designed for area defense against enemy aircraft. Whatever the merits of either, the controversy over the systems became another interservice controversy of the 1950s. In reality by 1959 both these systems were virtually obsolete, since the Soviet missile potential had kept improving. As for the longer lead-time Nike-Zeus, a hoped-for defense against enemy missiles, the army's request for $1 billion for 1959 (including funds for the production of long lead-time items) had not impressed Eisenhower who had reduced it to $300 million. The air force was supportive of this cut, declaring "the best defense is a good offense." However, Congress did eventually provide an extra $137 million that year for Zeus while cutting funds from the Bomarc program. Offensive missile developments were simply moving too fast in the late 1950s to solve the antimissile problem. Eisenhower seems to have sensed this and resisted successfully any attempt to go into production on an antimissile missile. SSAC, *Defense Appropriations, FY 1960*, 86/1, pp. 33, 309, 329, 330.

80. SSAC, *Defense Appropriations, FY 1960*, 86th Cong., 1st sess., 1959, pp. 100–104.

81. Ibid., pp. 200–202.

82. Ibid., pp. 262, 286.

83. *C.R.*, 86th Cong., 1st sess., vol. 105, pt. 7:9588 ff, 13177–79, 13194.

84. Ibid., p. 13256.

85. Ibid., p. 13300.

86. In some ways the most spectacular hearings that spring, though not related directly to the appropriation process, were those of Lyndon Johnson's Preparedness Subcommittee. There is no doubt that the hearings were politically embarrassing to the administration, and were so designed. There was no question, either, of the breakdown of public consensus within the administration, which had started earlier with the testimony of the army and navy's leadership in the House. There was unusual interest by the subcommittee in exactly how the Eisenhower defense budget had been developed. Budgetary ceilings, which had been denied, and the role of the Bureau of the Budget seemed to hold the greatest fascination for the senators. In retrospect, the effect of these hearings on the Eisenhower strategy and the defense budget was negligible. Probably the primary motivation for them was the 1960 presidential campaign. From that perspective, the hearings were perhaps successful, in that they were of some significance in setting the stage for the defense debate of the 1960 presidential campaign. For an interesting perspective on LBJ's revitalization and political use of this subcommittee commencing with Sputnik, see Reedy, *Twilight of the Presidency*, pp. 52 ff.

87. Note published in *U.S. Department of State Bulletin* (January 19, 1959), p. 81.

88. Horelick and Rush, *Strategic Power*, p. 117.

89. Jack M. Schick, *The Berlin Crisis, 1958–1962* (Philadelphia: University of Pennsylvania Press, 1971), p. 233.

90. Eisenhower, *Waging Peace*, p. 337; MCP, December 11, 1958. At one time Taylor had been commandant of the U.S. garrison in Berlin. This may explain why he represented the Joint Chiefs at this meeting.

91. On this point the British, according to Eisenhower (*Waging Peace*, p. 333), tended to be the most conciliatory of the allies. Some commentators, such as John Newhouse, feel that Macmillan was willing to pay a higher price than the other countries to defuse the situation (*De Gaulle and the Anglo Saxons*, pp. 90–93). De Gaulle, according to Newhouse, looked at Berlin as an opportunity for political maneuver for France and viewed Khrushchev's maneuvering as a bluff. Adenauer wanted no outcome that would infringe on the sovereignty of the Federal Republic, but probably was not keen on the use of force to keep open the ground corridor to Berlin.

92. "Declaration on Berlin," *NATO Facts and Figures* (Brussels: NATO Information Service, 1969), p. 332. The U.S. note is contained in U.S., Congress, Senate, Committee on Foreign Relations, *Documents on Germany, 1944–1970*, 92d Cong., 1st sess., 1971, pp. 379, 390. Schick, *Berlin Crisis*, p. 38.

93. Eisenhower, *Waging Peace*, p. 340; MCP, January 29, 1959.

94. The U.S. note is contained in *Documents on Germany*, p. 411. *Public Papers*, 1959, pp. 194, 217, 245.

95. Harold Macmillan, *Riding the Storm* (London: Macmillan, 1971), pp. 587–89.

96. Ibid., p. 683.

97. Eisenhower, *Waging Peace*, p. 347.

98. Ibid., p. 336 n.

99. *Public Papers*, 1959, pp. 273–82.

100. Although U.S. officials were not aware of it during the March meetings, Macmillan apparently had committed himself to a summit conference while he was in Moscow earlier. Lloyd later passed this on to Herter in Geneva, who included it in a cable to C. Douglas Dillon, undersecretary of state. When Dillon told this to Eisenhower, the president agreed it was a "shocking thing," but said Macmillan had intimated it to him at Camp David. Eisenhower added that this probably explained some of the British intransigence over the issue of East-West negotiations. MCP, June 15, 1959, March 21, 1959.

101. Macmillan, *Riding the Storm*, p. 647; MCP, July 2, 1959.

102. MCP, March 22, 1959.

103. Taking advantage of the 1958 amendments, Eisenhower subsequently sent a series of special messages to Congress transmitting proposed agreements to improve defense planning and training with the allies in nuclear matters. See, for example, *Public Papers*, 1959, p. 119.

104. MCP, February 8, 1960. There was subsequently created an Allied Command Europe Mobile Force for "showing the flag" on the NATO flanks; however, it was not atomic in the way Norstad implied it would be, but only potentially, in the way all NATO forces are—the United States controls the warheads.

105. MCP, August 19 and two on September 12, 1960.

106. Of course this could also be interpreted in another way. Eisenhower, having put his views into an earlier BNSP, was unwilling to alter them—thus he made light of the BNSP to his advantage.

CHAPTER FOUR

1. Eisenhower, *Mandate for Change*, pp. 446, 451.

2. John S. D. Eisenhower, unpublished manuscript (1972).

3. See for example Taylor, *Uncertain Trumpet*, p. 122.

4. Paul Hammond, *Organizing for Defense* (Princeton: Princeton University Press, 1961), p. 349.

5. Lewis Anthony Dexter, "Congressmen and the Making of Military Policy," in *Components of Defense Policy*, ed. Davis B. Bobrow (Chicago: Rand McNally, 1965), pp. 94–110; Huntington, *Common Defense*, pp. 123–46; Warner Schilling, "Fiscal 1950," in *Strategy, Politics, and Defense Budgets*, ed. Schilling, Hammond, and Snyder, pp. 245–49; Charles L. Schultze et al., eds., *Setting National Priorities: The 1973 Budget* (Washington, D.C.: Brookings, 1972), pp. 171–74.

6. Jackson, *National Security Council*, pp. 38, 39.

7. Eisenhower's success in domestic matters is another question. Peter Lyon refers to Eisenhower's "proud and prudent record in the conduct of foreign affairs" and his lack of "impressive successes" on the domestic scene in his conclusions; *Eisenhower*, p. 851.

# Bibliographical Essay

MANUSCRIPTS

The Eisenhower presidency is still close enough in time to limit access to the State Department files and certain other papers. However, there is a surprising amount of material available to the researcher, and I suspect when the now-closed papers are available there will be few, if any, dramatically new insights provided.

The following is not intended to be definitive but rather to record my research experience on this study. The starting point for manuscripts on the period is the Dwight D. Eisenhower Library in Abilene, Kansas, operated by the National Archives and Records Service of the General Services Administration. The director and his staff are very responsive to requests for information on holdings. Their booklet which lists materials in the library is helpful.

With regard to defense matters during Eisenhower's term of office the following manuscripts in Abilene listed under the name of an individual are especially useful, although certain portions of the papers are closed: Sherman Adams, Evan P. Aurand, Edward L. Beach, Robert Cutler, Joseph M. Dodge, Dwight D. Eisenhower, Bryce N. Harlow, Rowland R. Hughes, C. D. Jackson, Arthur Larson, Neil McElroy, Wilton B. Persons, Donald A. Quarles, and Maurice H. Stans. Other relevant manuscripts are public statements of the secretaries of defense, Draper Committee records, and records of the Staff secretary.

The papers of John Foster Dulles are contained in the Firestone Library at Princeton University. These are not the official papers of his period as secretary of state, which are under control of the State Department. Manuscripts relevant to his tenure as secretary contain articles, speeches, statements, testimony, interviews, reports, correspondence, clippings, photographs, memorabilia, and conference dossiers. Of these the latter, titled category IX, are the most useful for a researcher interested in defense matters. All quotations, citations, or references to the Dulles papers must be submitted to the reference librarian, in the context of their usage, prior to publication.

The Charles E. Wilson archives are at Anderson College, Anderson, Indiana. Papers pertaining to his period as secretary of defense are not extensive and not particularly significant. The public papers of George M. Humphrey have been compiled by Nathaniel R. Howard, *The Basic Papers of George M. Humphrey* (Cleveland, 1965).

Manuscripts in military service collections are in three locations: the air force in Montgomery, Alabama; the navy at the Washington Navy Yard; and the army at Carlisle Barracks, Pennsylvania. I had an opportunity to research the last two. The Naval History Division is especially cooperative in securing the declassification of documents (at least those from the 1950s) upon a researcher's request. The U.S. Army Military History Research Collection is especially noteworthy for a very extensive interview program of retired army leaders. Being located at the Army War College this program is able to use highly capable and knowledgeable student interviewers and expand their collection each year.

ORAL HISTORY

There are two oral history projects, at Princeton and Columbia, that are especially useful in studying the Eisenhower presidency. Oral history projects are valuable to a researcher and do save time. In certain areas though, they must be supplemented by interviews. This is especially true in matters of national security, where officials being interviewed for oral history projects tend to be overly cautious and sometimes feel they are under security restrictions even when they are not. When hearing all a researcher knows already, individuals are often inclined to be more free in their comments. Another problem with oral history is that it is only as good as its purpose and the individual doing the interviewing. Its purpose may not be the same as the researcher's— time and again I came across dropped questions by an interviewer unfamiliar with matters of national security. One final caution on oral history sources: The reader is dealing with perceptions of perceptions, that is, recall of what the person being interviewed believed he thought or did sometime in the past. Memories are selective and favorable about one's own past actions and in many cases about the past actions of the person who is the subject of the interview. For example, if one depended primarily on the Dulles Oral History Project for writing a biography of Dulles, there would be considerably fewer warts on the portrait than if one used that project as only an incidental research source.

The Dulles Oral History Project at Princeton has a relatively small number of transcripts which are closed or contain special restrictions. The most useful interviews for researching defense matters in the 1950s are those of Sherman Adams, Joseph Alsop, Dillon Anderson, Robert Bowie, Arleigh Burke, Lucius Clay, Dwight D. Eisenhower, Thomas Finletter, Thomas Gates, Andrew Goodpaster, Gordon Gray, Bryce Harlow, Christian Herter, Emmet Hughes, George Humphrey, John Irwin, George Kennan, Curtis LeMay, Peter Lisagor, Henry Cabot Lodge, Henry Luce, Neil McElroy, Richard Nixon, Lauris Norstad, Roderic O'Connor, Arthur Radford, Matthew Ridgway, Bernard Shanley, James

Shepley, Gerard Smith, Robert Sprague, Maxwell Taylor, Nathan Twining, and George Yeh.

In the Columbia Oral History Project both the interviewers and the focus are different. The focus is on Eisenhower rather than Dulles. Hence, although there will be repetition of names with the Dulles project the interviews are sufficiently different in most cases to warrant a researcher's time. The Columbia collection tends to have more restrictions than the Princeton collection. The following are most useful in researching defense matters (in the case of closed transcripts this is an assumption rather than a known fact): Sherman Adams, Joseph Alsop, Dillon Anderson, Edward Beach, Robert Bowie, Arleigh Burke, Lucius Clay, Charles Coolidge, Clarence Dillon, William Draper, Dwight D. Eisenhower, John Eisenhower, William Franke, Thomas Gates, Andrew Goodpaster, Gordon Gray, Alfred Gruenther, James Hagerty, Bryce Harlow, Roger Jones, James Killian (closed), Lyman Lemnitzer, Robert Lovett, John McCone, Neil McElroy, Nelson Rockefeller (closed), Robert Schulz, Dudley Sharp, Mansfield Sprague, Elmer Staats, Maurice Stans (closed), Lewis Strauss (closed), Robert Thayer, Nathan Twining.

PUBLIC DOCUMENTS

Congressional documents and the press are, at present, the best public sources of information on national security matters during the 1950s. For Congress the speeches and debates in the *Congressional Record* are useful to a point. Most of the congressional debates on defense during the 1950s shed more heat than light, yet they are useful in getting a diversity of rationales if one keeps in mind the various constituencies being addressed sometimes simultaneously—constituents, newspapers, and fellow senators to name the more common.

Probably more useful are the hearings by appropriations and legislative committees. The House Appropriations Subcommittee on Defense is probably more useful than the Senate subcommittee since its hearings occur first and there tends to be considerable repetition—although both can be used profitably. The Pentagon witnesses tend to stress House actions they are "appealing" to the Senate and sometimes new rationales develop. A very valuable aid to analyzing congressional actions on defense matters in the 1950s is Edward A. Kolodziej, *The Uncommon Defense and Congress, 1945–1963* (Columbus, Ohio, 1966).

Aside from appropriations committees, hearings of the Armed Services and Foreign Relations (Affairs) committees can be very useful on an issue basis. During the period after Sputnik and for the remainder of the Eisenhower administration, Lyndon Johnson's Preparedness Subcommittee of the Senate Armed Services Committee provided some interesting headlines and some insight into selected defense issues. Also Henry Jackson's Committee on Government Operations published some interesting material on the defense policy process from the perspective of late in the Eisenhower period. See *Organizing for National Security—Selected Materials, The Bureau of the Budget and the Budgetary Process,* and *The National Security Council.* These publications— especially the latter document—tend to be a bit simplistic and are worded in such a way that one tends to forget their partisan nature. An annual congressional document unique to the second Eisenhower term is Charles H. Donnelly, *United States Defense Policies since World War II* (Washington, D.C., 1957–1961). These assist in identifying the major defense issues of the period.

There are two public documents emanating from the executive branch of considerable value to a researcher of the 1950s. First is the National Archives and Records Service's *Public Papers of the Presidents of the United States* (Washington, D.C., 1953–1960). The other is the unique *Pentagon Papers.* Whatever their limitations, and there are many, in evaluating the war in Vietnam, they nevertheless are a useful source of original documentation for a researcher of the Eisenhower period. I used the Gravel edition (Boston, 1971), in which volume one covers the period from 1940 to 1960. Especially valuable is Document 18, pp. 412–29, which outlines the strategic thinking of Eisenhower at the time of the launching of the New Look. The Gravel edition volume five—a supplement—is indispensable not because of the critical essays it contains but because it contains name and subject indexes to volumes one through four.

I used two newspapers in the course of this study, the *New York Times* and the *Washington Post*. In the *Times*, the editorial page shifted on Eisenhower depending on the defense issue and there was a sufficient variety of columnists to get pro and con comments on the president. The *Washington Post* was an especially good supplement to the *New York Times*. In those days it had a small-town flavor to it, but in this case the small town was Washington and it was especially good in providing insights into the capital political scene. In general, Eisenhower received quite good press support in his first term which, however, fell off quite sharply soon after the start of his second term.

SECONDARY LITERATURE

Writings about the Eisenhower presidency began relatively early in his administration and in various forms continued through the conclusion of his term of office. After a hiatus of several years they have resumed. Only selected writings of interest to those researching in defense matters during the period are listed. Some of this literature is not directly related to defense issues but rather serves to place such issues in the perspective of the Eisenhower period.

*Memoirs:* Edward Crankshaw, *Khrushchev Remembers* (New York: Bantam, 1971); Dwight Eisenhower, *Mandate for Change* (New York: Doubleday, 1963); *Waging Peace* (New York: Doubleday, 1965); John Eisenhower, *Strictly Personal* (New York: Doubleday, 1974); George Kennan, *Memoirs*, vol. II (Boston: Little, Brown, 1972) ; Harold Macmillan, *Riding the Storm* (New York: Harper, 1971); Richard Nixon, *Six Crises* (New York: Doubleday, 1962).

*Insiders:* Sherman Adams, *First-Hand Report* (New York: Harper, 1961); Dillon Anderson, "The President and National Security," *Atlantic* (January 1956); Robert Cutler, *No Time for Rest* (Boston: Little, Brown, 1966); Emmet Hughes, *The Ordeal of Power* (New York: Athene:ım, 1963); Arthur Larson, *Eisenhower, the President Nobody Knew* (New York: Popular Library, 1968); Lewis Strauss, *Men and Decisions* (New York: Doubleday, 1962).

*Early Writings on the Eisenhower Administration:* Marquis Childs, *Eisenhower Captive Here* (New York: Harcourt Brace, 1958); Robert Donovan, *Eisenhower: The Inside Story* (New York: Harper, 1956); Norman Graebner, "Eisenhower's Popular Leadership," *Current History* (October 1960); Sidney Hyman, "The Failure of the Eisenhower Presidency," *Progressive* (May 1960); Richard Neustadt, *Presidential Power* (New York: Wiley, 1960); Merlo Pusey, *Eisenhower the President* (New York: Macmillan, 1956); Richard Rovere, *Affairs of State: The Eisenhower Years* (New York: Farrar, Strauss and Cudahy, 1956); William Shannon, "Eisenhower as President," *Commentary* (November 1958); Merriman Smith, *Meet Mister Eisenhower* (New York: Harper, 1954), and *A President's Odyssey* (New York: Harper, 1961).

*Defense Related Matters during the Eisenhower Administration:* Michael H. Armacost, *The Politics of Weapons Innovation: The Thor-Jupiter Controversy* (New York: Columbia University Press, 1969); P. M. S. Blackett, *Atomic Weapons and East-West Relations* (Cambridge: Cambridge University Press, 1956); Bernard Brodie, *Strategy in the Missile Age* (Princeton, N.J.: Princeton University Press, 1959); Edgar M. Bottome, *The Missile Gap* (Rutherford, N.J.: Fairleigh Dickinson University Press, 1971); Seyom Brown, *The Faces of Power* (New York: Columbia University Press, 1968); David B. Capitanchik, *The Eisenhower Presidency and American Foreign Policy* (London: Routledge and Kegan Paul, 1969); Herbert S. Dinerstein, *Fifty Years of Soviet Foreign Policy* (Baltimore, Md.: Johns Hopkins Press, 1968); Allen Dulles, *The Craft of Intelligence* (New York: Harper and Row, 1963); Eugene M. Emme, ed., *The Impact of Air Power*

158   *Bibliographical Essay*

(New York: Van Nostrand, 1959); Alain C. Enthoven and K. Wayne Smith, *How Much Is Enough?* (New York: Harper and Row, 1971); James M. Gavin, *War and Peace in the Space Age* (New York: Harper, 1958); Louis L. Gerson, *John Foster Dulles* (New York: Cooper Square, 1967); Richard Goold-Adams, *John Foster Dulles: A Reappraisal* (New York: Appleton-Century-Crofts, 1962); Michael A. Guhin, *John Foster Dulles: A Statesman and His Times* (New York: Columbia University Press, 1972); Louis J. Halle, *The Cold War as History* (New York: Harper and Row, 1967); Morton H. Halperin, *Limited War: An Annotated Bibliography* (Cambridge, Mass.: Harvard Center for International Affairs, 1962); Paul Y. Hammond, *Organizing for Defense* (Princeton, N.J.: Princeton University Press, 1961); Townsend Hoopes, *The Devil and John Foster Dulles* (Boston: Little, Brown, 1973); Arnold L. Horelick and Myron Rush, *Strategic Power and Soviet Foreign Policy* (Chicago: University of Chicago Press, 1965); Samuel P. Huntington, *The Common Defense* (New York: Columbia University Press, 1961); Henry M. Jackson, ed., *The National Security Council* (New York: Praeger, 1965); William W. Kaufmann, ed., *Military Policy and National Security* (Princeton, N.J.: Princeton University Press, 1956); Henry A. Kissinger, *Nuclear Weapon and Foreign Policy* (New York: Harper, 1957); Klaus Knorr, *NATO and American Security* (Princeton, N.J.: Princeton University Press, 1959); Oskar Morgenstern, *The Question of National Defense* (New York: Random House, 1959); Richard O. Neville, "The United States Army: Strategic Doctrine and Political Role" (Honors thesis, Harvard College, 1958); Robert E. Osgood, *Limited War* (Chicago: Chicago University Press, 1957), and *NATO: The Entangling Alliance* (Chicago: Chicago University Press, 1962); Paul Peeters, *Massive Retaliation* (Chicago: Henry Regnery, 1959); George H. Quester, *Nuclear Diplomacy* (New York: Dunellen, 1970); Matthew B. Ridgway, *Soldier* (New York: Harper, 1956); Rockefeller Brothers Fund, Report of Panel II, *International Security: The Military Aspect* (New York: Doubleday, 1958); W. W. Rostow, *The United States in the World Arena* (New York:

Simon and Schuster, 1960); Jack M. Schick, *The Berlin Crisis, 1958–1962* (Philadelphia: University of Pennsylvania Press, 1971); Sir John Slessor, *The Great Deterrent* (New York: Praeger, 1957); Dale O. Smith, *U.S. Military Doctrine* (New York: Duell, Sloan, and Pearce, 1955) ; William P. Snyder, *The Politics of British Defense Policy, 1945–1962* (Columbus: Ohio State University Press, 1964); Harold Stein, ed., *American Civil-Military Decisions: A Book of Case Studies* (University: University of Alabama Press, 1963); Maxwell D. Taylor, *The Uncertain Trumpet* (New York: Harper, 1959); Nathan F. Twining, *Neither Liberty nor Safety* (New York: Holt, Rinehart, and Winston, 1966); A. J. Wohlstetter et al., *Selection and Use of Strategic Air Bases* (New York: Rand Corporation, 1954); Thomas W. Wolfe, *Soviet Strategy at the Crossroads* (Cambridge, Mass.: Harvard University Press, 1964).

*Articles:* Lloyd V. Berkner, "Continental Defense," *Current History* (May 1954); Alvin J. Cottrell and James E. Dougherty, "Nuclear Weapons, Policy and Strategy," *Orbis* (Summer 1957); Robert Cutler, "The Development of the National Security Council," *Foreign Affairs* (April 1956); John Davenport, "Arms and the Welfare State," *Yale Review* (March 1958); Raymond H. Dawson, "Congressional Innovation and Intervention in Defense Policy," *American Political Science Review* (March 1962); Bernard K. Gordon, "The Military Budget: Congressional Phase," *Journal of Politics* (November 1961); Morton H. Halperin, "The Gaither Committee and the Policy Process," *World Politics* (April 1961); Seymour E. Harris, "The Battle of the Budget," *Current History* (May 1954); Malcolm W. Hoag, "Some Complexities in Military Planning," *World Politics* (July 1959); Samuel P. Huntington, "The Separation of Powers: Dual Control over the National Forces," *American Political Science Review* (September 1956), and "Strategic Planning and the Political Process," *Foreign Affairs* (January 1960); Henry M. Jackson, "Organizing for Survival," *Foreign Affairs* (April 1960); Arnold Kanter, "Congress and the Defense Budget," *American Political Science Review* (March 1972); James E. King, "Limited Defense" and "Limited Annihilation?" Review of *Nuclear Weapons and Foreign Policy* by Henry Kissinger, *New Republic* (July 1 and 15, 1957); G. A. Lincoln and Amos A. Jordan, "Technology and the Changing Nature of General War," *Military Review* (May 1957); David Demarest Lloyd, "The Sham Battle over Spending," *Reporter* (January 8, 1959); Charles J. V. Murphy, a series of eighteen articles on the Eisenhower administration's defense policies in *Fortune*, beginning in August 1953 and ending in November 1959; Richard E. Neustadt, "Presidency and Legislation: Planning the President's Program," *American Political Science Review* (December 1955); Paul H. Nitze, "Atoms, Strategy, and Policy," *Foreign Affairs* (January 1956); E. Raymond Platig, "The 'New Look' Raises Old Problems," *Review of Politics* (January 1955); Richard H. Rovere, "Eisenhower over the Shoulder," *American Scholar* (Spring 1962); Sir John Slessor, "Air Power and World Strategy," *Foreign Affairs* (October 1954); Edward Teller, "Alternatives for Security," *Foreign Affairs* (January 1958); James Tobin, "Defense, Dollars, and Doctrines," *Yale Review* (March 1958; Albert Wohlstetter, "The Delicate Balance of Terror," *Foreign Affairs* (January 1959); Arnold Wolfers, "Europe and the NATO Shield," *International Organization* (Autumn 1958); Richard A. Yudkin, "American Armed Strength and Its Influence," *Annals* (July 1969).

*Recent Writings concerning the Eisenhower Administration:* Charles Alexander, *Holding the Line: The Eisenhower Era, 1952–1961* (Bloomington: Indiana University Press, 1975); Martin Herz, *Beginnings of the Cold War* (New York: McGraw Hill, 1969); Murray Kempton, "The Underestimation of Dwight D. Eisenhower," *Esquire* (September 1967); Joyce and Gabriel Kolko, *The Limits of Power* (New York: Harper and Row, 1972); John Leo, "Dwight David Eisenhower: Ranking an Ex-President," *Commonweal* (April 11, 1969); Peter Lyon, *Eisenhower: Portrait of the Hero* (Boston: Little, Brown, 1974); Herbert Parmet, *Eisenhower and the American Crusades* (New York: Macmillan, 1972); George Reedy, *The Twilight of the Presidency* (Boston: Houghton Mifflin, 1973).

# Index

Acheson, Dean, 16; as critic, 112
Adams, Sherman, 18, 19, 20, 28, 40, 67
Adenauer, Konrad, 113; and Berlin situation, 110; visit from Dulles, 112
AEC (Atomic Energy Commission), 59; John McCone, chairman of, 118
aggression: Korean type, 96; Lebanese type, 96
air force, 5, 29, 43, 59, 62, 77, 117; as beneficiary of budget increases, 86; Bomarc, 106; on bombers, 60; budget, 63, 106; chairman, 55; chief of staff, 6, 23, 116; chiefs, 74–75, 131, 135; critics of, 60; efforts for funds, 48; excess of strategic weapons, 103; funds, 56, 98, 103; Jupiter, 82; leaders, testimony of, 103; on limited war, 103–4; missile program, 79, 88; modernization, 49, 75; and publicity, 53; Radford's testimony on behalf of, 30; strategic concepts, 23; strategic missile program, 98; strategic retaliatory force, 98; strength of, 23; and Stuart Symington, 5

airlift adequacy, 98, 103
Air National Guard, 31
allies, 14, 36, 40, 70; closure of Berlin to, 108–9; domestic scene, 126; intelligence, 49; invulnerability, challenge to, 119; people, 11, 14, 85, 117; position relative to Soviet Union, 109; proconsul in Europe, 118; public, speeches to, 81; release of warheads to, 71; writers, 39
Anderson, Robert B., 72; successor to Humphrey, 129
Arab world, 39
army, 24, 29, 30, 31, 32, 43, 115; aerial reconnaissance, 51; and air defense, 77; antimissile missile, 97; aviation and missiles, 52; budget, 57–58, 63, 105; chief of staff, 2, 22, 41; and Defense Department, 84; divisions, 34; efforts for funds, 48; goal, 78; inventory, 97; leaders, 48, 58, 117; in limited war, 49, 56; missile agency, 82; modernization of, 56, 88, 96, 107; Nike-Hercules, 106; Nike-Zeus, 106; in nuclear war, 56; personnel strength of, 88, 101, 103; reservations on budget,

recession of 1957–1958, 66, 67
Reorganization Act of 1958, 93
Republican: campaign of 1952, 10,
    11, 19; congressional leaders, 3,
    6; foreign policy platform, 124;
    image, 67; majority, 28, 38; party,
    2, 67; platform, 12: program, 5;
    spokesman for party, 17; success
    of party, 3; views on managing
    the economy, 7
Republicans: congressional, 68;
    conservative, 132
Ridgway, General Matthew B., 22,
    25, 26, 30, 32, 34, 35, 41, 42;
    memoirs of, 54
righteous peace, 11
Riley, Congressman John, 99
Rockefeller Committee on Govern-
    mental Organization, 89
Roosevelt, Franklin D., 29
Russell, Vice Chief James, 105
Russia. *See* Soviet Union

SAC (Strategic Air Command), 56,
    75, 77, 79, 85
Saltonstall, Senator Leverett, 107
"Science and National Security"
    (Eisenhower speech), 82
secretary of defense, 20, 21, 42, 116,
    127; authority of, 91; military
    advice to, 130
secretary of state, 18, 116
secretary of the treasury, 19, 20, 116
Senate, 28, 33, 34, 56; appropriation
    hearings, 32; Armed Services
    Committee, 50, 92; defense ap-
    propriations hearings, 104; floor
    debate, 35, 107; Foreign Relations
    Committee, 33; Republican lead-
    er of, 3
SHAPE, 22, 124
ship modernization, 59
Sikes, Robert L. F., 29, 30, 31, 32,
    100, 103
Smith, Gerard, 86, 88, 114
Southeast Asia, 34
Soviet Union, 6, 10, 11, 13, 23, 39,
    68, 70; accomplishment, 79; ac-
    tion against the allies, 109, 114;
    advanced aircraft, 49; aggression,
    14; American and NATO posi-
    tions relative to, 109; -American

relationships, 10; answer to note,
    112; antiaircraft defenses, 79;
    army, 10; Aviation Day, 38; ca-
    pabilities, 39, 94, 120; capability
    for local war, 86; challenge over
    Berlin, 66; and the cold war, 109;
    competition between the United
    States and, 96; conflict between
    the United States and, 117, 119;
    and conventional war, 64, 111;
    dealing with, 112; defense spend-
    ing, 105; deployed missiles, 85;
    détente with, 47; deterrence of,
    71; forces, potential contact with,
    115; foreign policy, 6; hydrogen
    bomb, 141 n. 64; hydrogen de-
    vice, 10; ICBM program, 68, 80,
    84; intentions, 69, 71, 124; launch-
    ing of Sputnik, 68; launchings,
    anxiety over, 81; leaders, 12, 38,
    39, 69, 109; lead in bombers, 39;
    massive retaliation, 81; military
    capabilities, 8, 10, 22, 35, 124;
    missiles, 70, 94; navy, 10; note,
    110; nuclear capability of, 57;
    orbiting of Sputnik, 76; peril of,
    124; periphery, 10; power, areas
    remote from, 116; pressures from,
    86; program for action, 17; prog-
    ress in bombers and missiles,
    50; satellite, 46; seaborne missiles,
    47; signing a peace treaty, 108;
    soldiers, 45; space achievements,
    68; sponsored military action, 13;
    strategic air force, 10; strategic
    capabilities, 75; strategic deliv-
    ery, 69; strategic hardware, 87;
    strategic posture, 6; strategic
    threat, 77; strategic weapons, 119;
    strategy, 13; subversion, 86; suc-
    cess, view of, 119; superiority
    over, 125; tactical air force, 10;
    technological gains, 68; tech-
    nological potential, 46; threat, 8,
    11; thrust, assertive, 66; ultima-
    tum, 112; visit by Macmillan,
    113; war involving the, 54, 55,
    116; weapons development, 87
Sprague, Robert, 20
Sputnik, 46, 67, 68, 70, 73–79, 84,
    117, 119, 125; changes brought

Sputnik *(continued)*:
about by, 120; impetus of, 89; launching of, 66
Stalin, 5, 10; successors to, 10
Stans, Maurice, 95, 96
State Department, 6; paper, 115; secretary, 135
State of the Union message, 26, 98
Stevens, Robert (secretary of the army), 30
Stevenson, Adlai, 2, 37
strategic: air force, 80; air power, 99; nuclear weapons, 64; parity, 127; policy, 69; policymaking and management of, 136; policy of Eisenhower, 123, 127; policy of the United States, 135
Subcommittee on National Policy Machinery, 133
Suez crisis, 39
Supreme Allied Commander in Europe, 118, 123
Supreme Command AEF, 1
Supreme Commander, 2, 13
Symington, Senator Stuart, 5, 50, 94, 105; Air Power Hearing Report, 59

Tactical Air Command, 75
tactical atomic weapons, 87
tactical nuclear weapons, 45, 64, 117
Taft, Senator Robert A., 2, 3, 12, 137 n. 1; efforts of, 132; as "Mr. Republican," 3
Taiwan, carriers used in, 95
Talbott, Harold (secretary of the air force), 31
Tass, press release from, 110
tax cut, 67
Taylor, General Maxwell, 41, 42, 52, 55, 56, 78, 82, 83, 87, 88, 96, 100, 102, 103, 105, 106, 109, 117; as army chief of staff, 51, 58; position of, 117; service chief, 72; strategic policy adversary, 121
Thomas, Charles (secretary of the navy), 42
Thor, air force, 85
Thor-Jupiter program, 85
Titan ICBM, 79
treasury, secretary of the, 15, 135

Treasury, United States, 19
Truman, Harry S., 1, 13, 14, 15, 16; administration, 7, 12, 17, 21, 126, 141 n. 64; budget, 3, 5; containment policy of, 124; period, 68; strategic legacy, 7; strategy, 126
Twining, General Nathan F., 22, 27, 60, 74, 82, 87, 92, 95, 96, 100, 101, 102, 103, 105, 110, 111, 113, 114

U-2 photography, 69
UN San Francisco Conference (1945), 17
United States, 6, 9, 10, 11, 12, 39, 44, 124; agreement with Great Britain and France, 118; air and sea support, 86; air force, 55; army, 47, 64; atomic arsenal, 13, 36, 71; budget, 36; capabilities, 44, 103; capabilities for limited war, 104, 114; competition between the Soviet Union and, 96; conflict between the Soviet Union and, 114, 117; credibility, 115; in crisis, 96; decision to deploy IRBMs, 109; defense commitment, 35; defense policy, 6, 35, 38, 43; defense posture, 30; defense programs, range of, 80; defenses, state of, 113; deterrent, 13, 14, 69, 86; domestic audience, 44; economy, 7, 47, 62, 63, 127, 135; emphasis on strategic power, 45; enemy bomber threats to, 97; exposed to Soviets, 85; forces, 69, 104, 112; force structure, 115; ground forces, 26; interests and objectives, 16; land forces, 55; leadership, 10, 119; and massive retaliation, 81; military commitments, 22; military missile effort, 76, 125; military position, 51; military posture, 75, 130; missile lag, 94; national security, 14; naval force, 10, 47, 55; need for conventional capabilities, 58; nuclear capability, 6; overall capability, 68; press, 68; resources, 103–4; response to Sputnik, 70; retaliatory capability, 106; scientific effort, 76; seaborne missiles

# The Author

Douglas Kinnard was a brigadier general in the U.S. Army when he elected to take early retirement and join the Princeton Department of Politics, where he received a Ph.D. in 1973. He taught political science at the University of Vermont until 1984 (he is now professor emeritus), served as U.S. Army chief of military history from 1983–84, and is presently Secretary of the Navy Senior Research Fellow at the Navy War College. Dr. Kinnard is the author of *The Secretary of Defense* (1980) and *The War Managers* (1985).